Butterflies Up Close
A Guide to Butterfly Photography

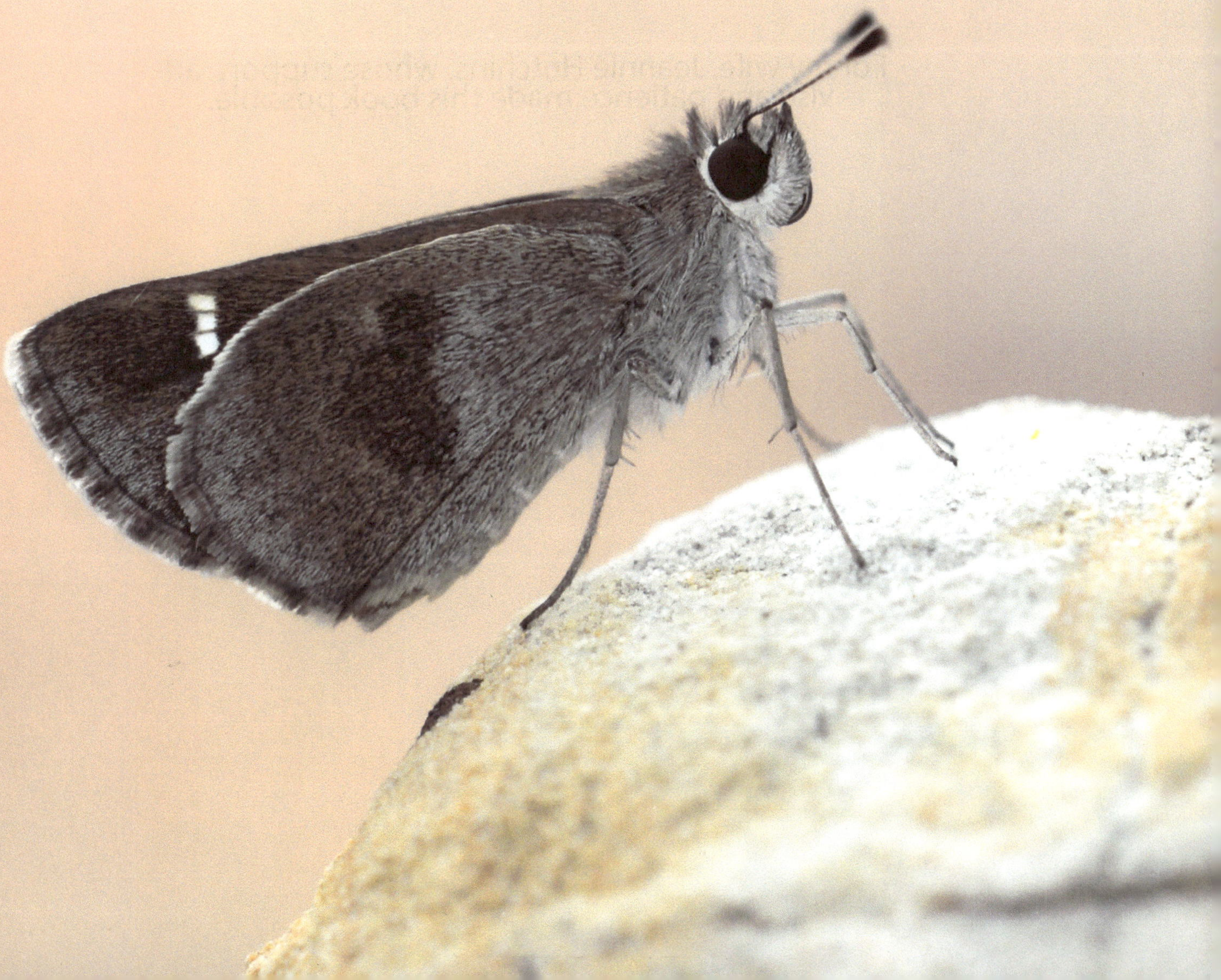

For my wife, Jeannie Hutchins, whose support, advise and patience made this book possible.

Butterflies Up Close
A Guide to Butterfly Photography

Roger Rittmaster, M.D.

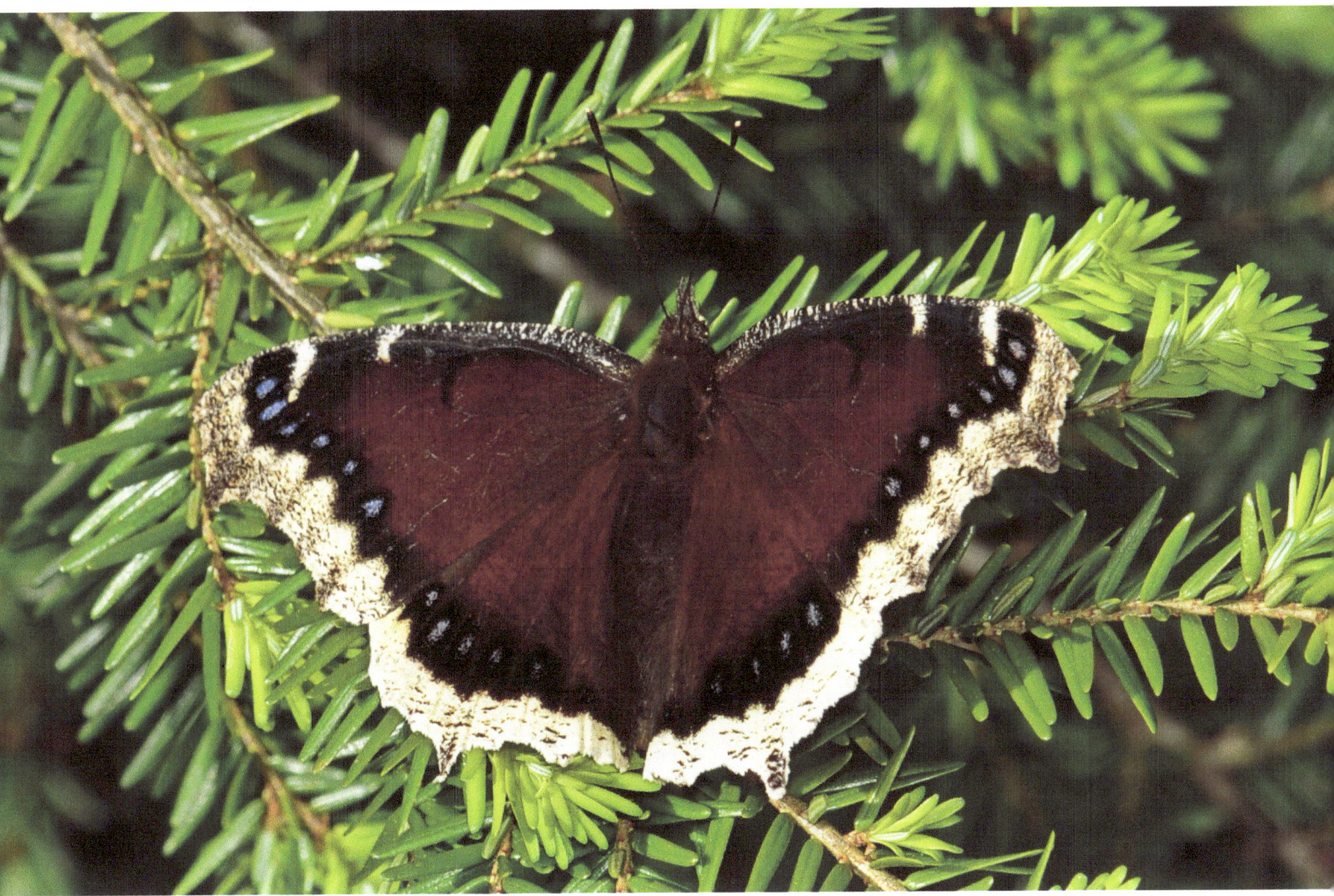

Rittmaster Consulting LLC, Publisher
2013

Cover Photo: Pipevine Swallowtail (*Battus philenor*)

Frontispiece Photo: Olive-clouded Skipper (*Lerodea arabus*)

Overleaf Photo: Mourning Cloak (*Nyphalis antiopa*)

First Printing: 2014

ISBN 978-0-9912802-0-9

Rittmaster Consulting LLC, Publisher
42 William Glen Drive
Camden, Maine 04843 USA
roger.rittmaster@gmail.com

Ordering Information:
Special discounts are available on quantity purchases by corporations,
associations, educators, and others. For details, contact the author at
the above listed address.

Contents

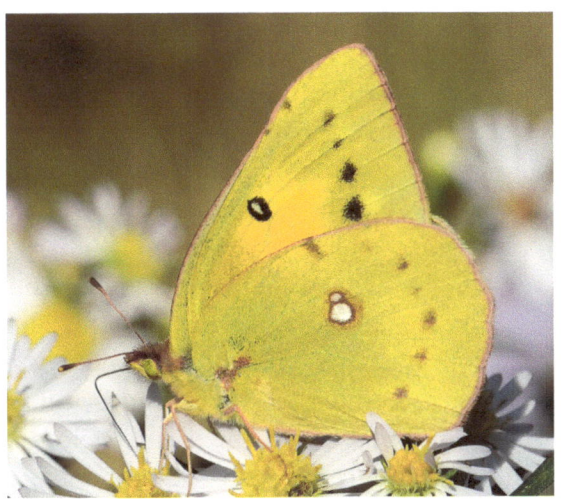

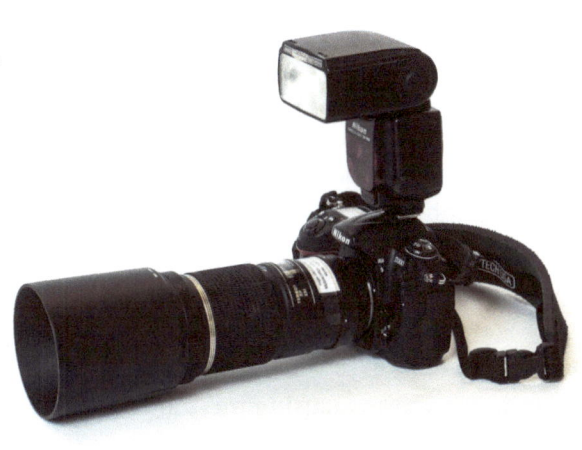

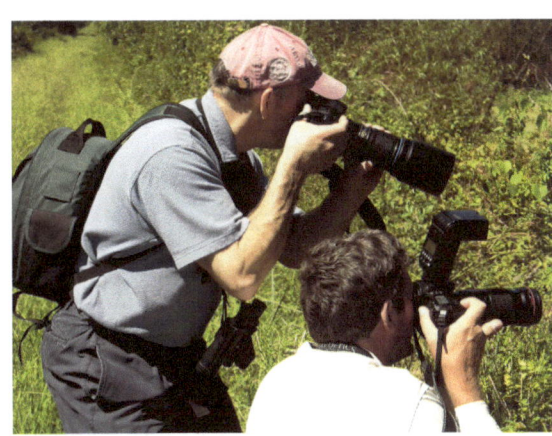

Preface

The beauty of butterflies, alone and in association with flowers, creates stunning opportunities for the nature photographer. The purpose of this book is to provide tips for finding and capturing this beauty. Although most of the images in this book are of butterflies, the techniques can equally be applied to other insects such as dragonflies and damselflies, which are equally striking. The book is written for photographers who want to expand their subject matter to butterflies and other insects, and to the butterfly enthusiasts who want to improve their ability to capture the beauty of what they see. The book will cover not only techniques and equipment, but also the composition and quality of the final image. However, this is not a book about the basics of photography – there are many such guides around, both in print and on the Web. The reader should already have an understanding of terms such as aperture, F-stop, ISO and shutter speed.

In one sense (at least!), this book is outdated the moment it is printed. Advances in cameras, lenses and flashes are so rapid that it would be foolhardy to focus on the details of particular systems. Furthermore, the ideal system doesn't exist: one that will provide a good depth of field with a pleasingly blurred background and that is so good at collecting light, that even the wings of a hovering butterfly can be frozen with superfast shutter speeds. Nevertheless, excellent photos can be taken with a variety of systems, each with its own strengths and weaknesses. I will attempt to explain how to get the most out of the camera system you are using. But beware, if you become addicted to the search for the prefect photo, you will inevitably be drawn towards the financial hole of progressively better equipment and more exotic travel locations.

Although I have taken butterfly photographs in many parts of the world, I've only used photographs from the United States and Canada in this book. The reason for this is that my best photographs are from North America. Not only have I spent much more time here, but also, when photographing butterflies abroad, I have been interested mainly in documenting what I've seen. In North America, I am seeking the perfect butterfly photograph.

A few words about my equipment… I started digital butterfly photography in 2000 with a Nikon Coolpix 990 and switched to a Coolpix 8700 with a Nikon SB-30 flash in 2004, soon after it became available (both point and shoot cameras). I was delighted with the quality of the close-up images I could take with the Coolpix 8700, but was frustrated with the number of photographs that I missed because of the need to get close and the slowness of the focusing mechanism. In 2009 I switched to a digital single lens reflex camera (Nikon D300) and shortly thereafter acquired a Tamron 180 mm macro lens. All photographs taken with the D300 camera used the Tamron telephoto macro lens. I've used different flashes over the years and currently use a Nikon Speedlight SB-900. All of this equipment is discussed in the text, along with the pros and cons of each. My preference for the Nikon line is historical: I have some excellent manual Nikon lens from as far back as the 1970's and still use them on occasion.

The recommendations in this book are specific for close-up insect photography. Although some of the techniques are applicable to a broad range of photography, others would be inappropriate for landscape or portrait photography, for example.

Thanks go to the many photographers with whom I have been able to share knowledge and ideas. I would especially like to thank the three North Carolina photographers that helped me get started: Randy Emmitt, Will Cook and Jeff Pippen. I would also like to thank the individuals who have reviewed parts or all of this book at its various stages: Robert Behrstock, Reid Elem, Mark Hengesbaugh, Gary Jue, and my wife, Jeannie Hutchins. Jeannie is an accomplished photographer in her own right and was the sounding board for many of the ideas in this book. She also tolerated and encouraged the hours and days I've spent in the field and at my computer.

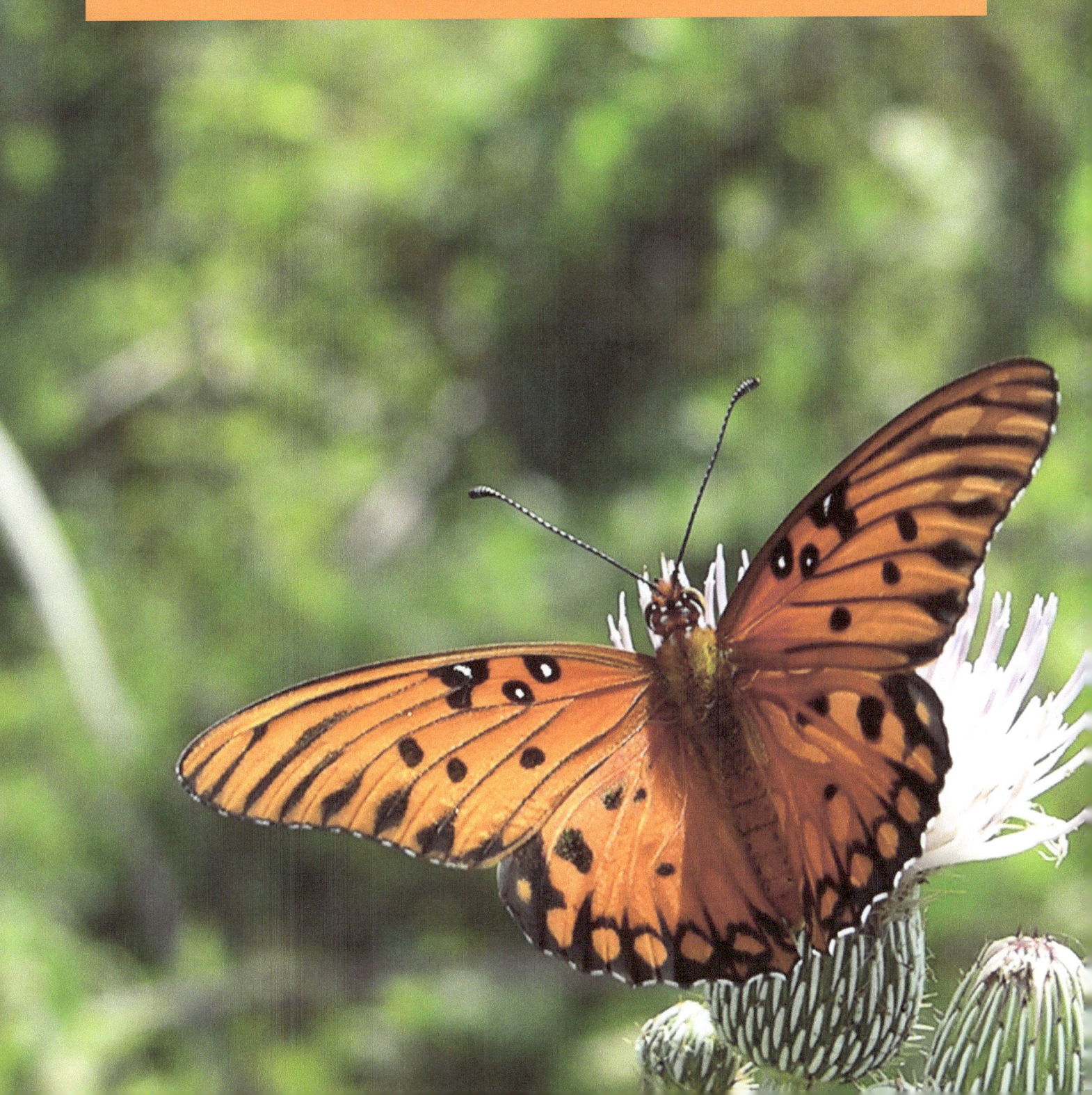

Section 1
Butterflies as Subjects

Why Photograph Butterflies?

Butterflies are among the most beautiful insects, and they often can be found on equally pretty flowers. Beyond capturing their beauty, photos can serve as a memory aid and means to identify unknown species. The better the photograph, the easier it will be to identify the butterfly. Even if one doesn't have friends who are experts in butterfly identification, there are now many books and websites that can help (see Pages 21-23 for some of these) and local butterfly clubs abound, either as independent organizations or clubs affiliated with the North American Butterfly Association (NABA; http://www.naba.org/chapters.html).

The desire to learn the names of butterflies inevitably leads to a desire to understand its natural history. When does a particular species fly? What is its behavior and when is it most likely to stay still enough for a photograph? What is its host plant (the plant on which its caterpillar feeds)? What does its caterpillar look like? How does it spend the winter? How can I attract it to my garden? Photographs can help to answer (or remember the answer to) many of these questions.

Photographs can also become teaching aids. In medicine there is an expression: "See one, do one, teach one" as a humorous acknowledgement of the rapidity with which one can go from student to practitioner to teacher. I find one of the best ways to enhance a field trip is to show photographs of what the participants are likely to see, find the butterflies in the field, and then review the photographs afterwards to solidify the learning experience.

But what if you only want to photograph butterflies for their beauty and don't care about their identification or natural history? Fine, but for most of us, that stage doesn't last very long. The first time you see a Black Swallowtail land on your parsley, fennel or dill plant, and then real-

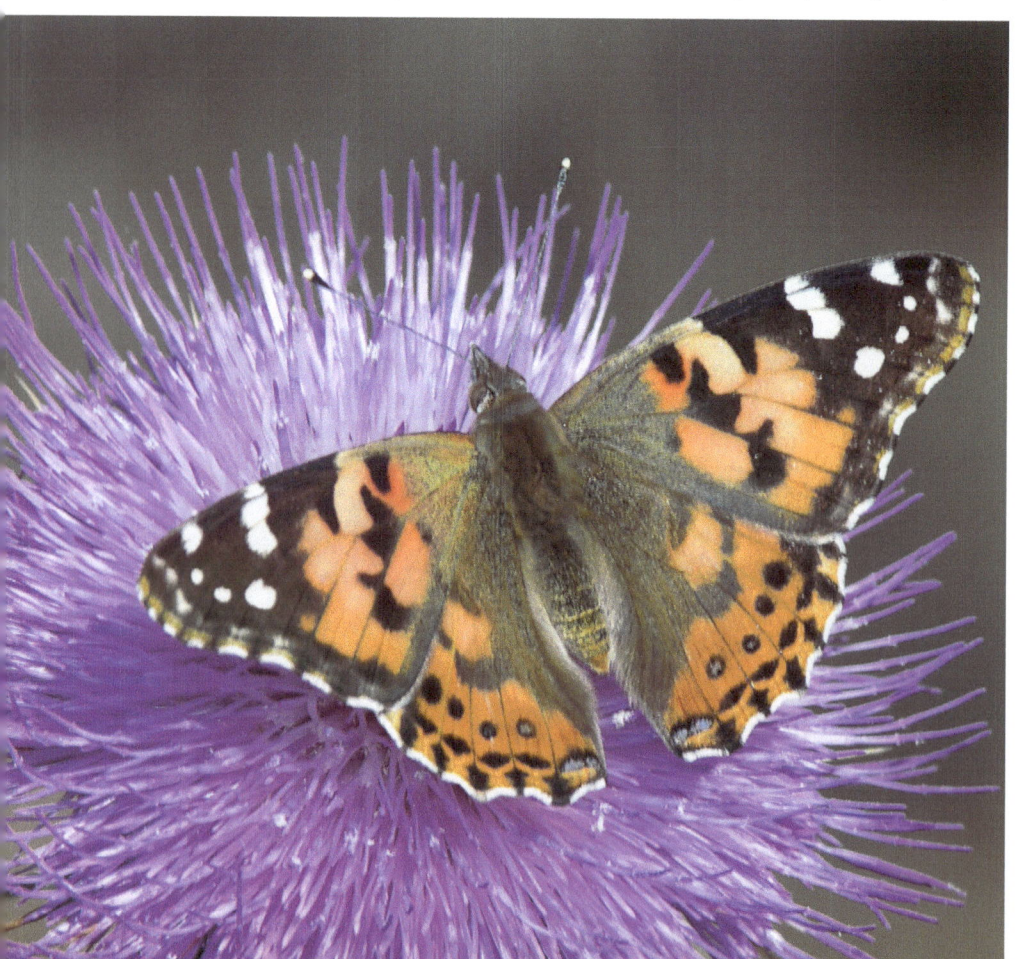

Painted Lady (*Vanessa cardui*) nectaring on one of its host plants, Arizona Thistle (*Cirsium arizonicum*). Photo taken in Sabino Canyon, Tucson, Arizona. Nikon Coolpix 8700 camera, ISO 50, F5.9, 1/370 sec.

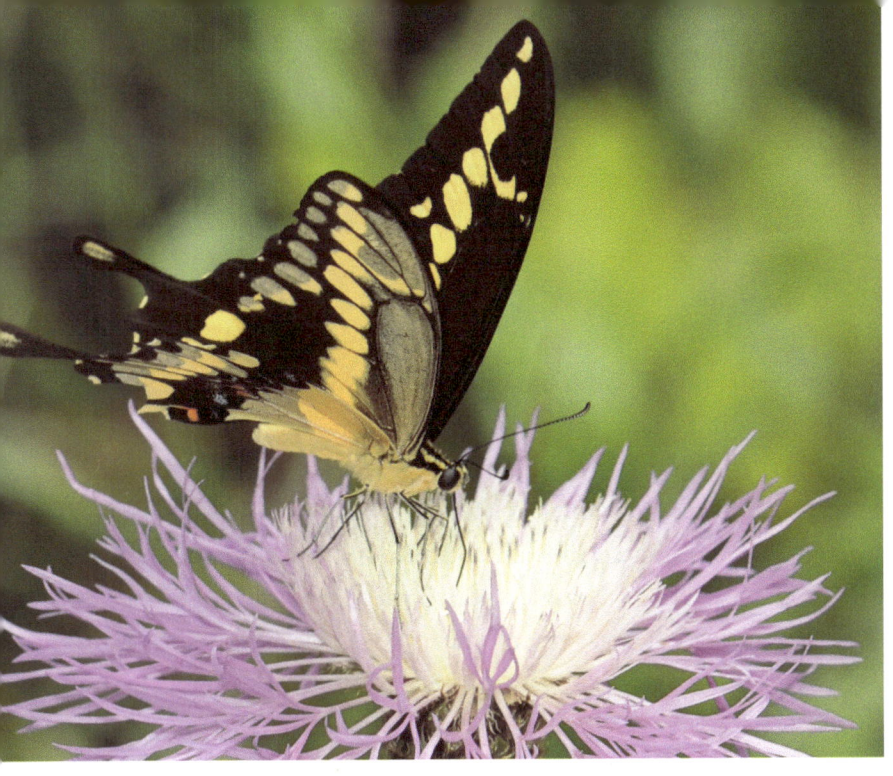

ize that those "pest" caterpillars belong to that Swallowtail, your appreciation and approach to photographing these beautiful animals may change forever. If you know the natural history of a butterfly, you'll have a better idea of where and when you are likely to find it. Regardless, you can ignore the natural history references in this book, and focus on the technical aspects of producing a great butterfly photograph.

Of course, we can't ignore the challenges. Butterflies have wings and use then to avoid predators. They are easy spooked, and ones that visit flowers often hop rapidly between flowers. The same syncopated flight patterns that help them avoid predation make them difficult to photograph on the wing. When a butterfly lands with its wings folded it is usually best to have the plane of the wings parallel to the cameras sensor, so that all of the wing will be in focus. However, given that a sphere is made up of an infinite number of two-dimensional planes, it is frustratingly common, by chance, for a butterfly to land in an orientation that is unsuitable for a good photograph. This book will highlight ways to overcome these challenges, but if you are short on patience, you might think about a different hobby.

Butterfly Photography Etiquette

Butterfly photographers sometimes have a spiritual appreciation of the beauty of their subjects. On the other hand, sometimes they stalk their quarry much as a hunter stalks a deer. And just as deer hunters prefer to hunt alone or perhaps with one other friend, the same is often true of butterfly photographers. Part of the reason is that it is much harder to get a good photo of a butterfly with a group of people milling about. But let's say you're on a guided tour to see a

Butterfly photography in pairs works best when both photographers have the same length telephoto lenses. In that manner they can stand a similar distance from the butterfly and stay far enough away not to scare the insect.

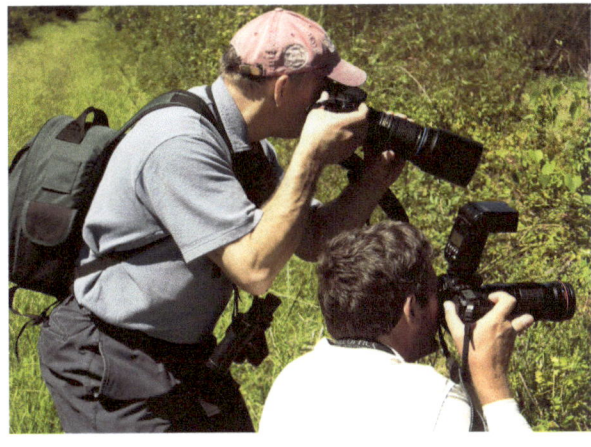

rare butterfly that you have never seen before. PLEASE let everyone in the group have a good look at the butterfly through binoculars, before you try to move in for a photo. If you rush in to capture the image, you'll irritate everyone in the group and probably scare the butterfly away. If there are just two people, it helps to set up ground rules in advance. The worst situation is when one person is about to click the shutter release, and his/her companion moves, or steps on a branch, and scares the butterfly away. Also, one must have respect for the environment, whether it be a botanical garden or a farmer's field. Care should be taken not to trample flowers or other vegetation while trying to line up the perfect angle for a photo.

Natural History of Butterflies

There are over 700 species of butterflies in the United States and Canada with new species occurring as rare vagrants are spotted flying north from Mexico. The exact number of species frequently changes as individual species are split or merged based on the consensus of butterfly experts. Of course, the experts don't always agree on what constitutes a given species, with the "splitters" stressing subtle differences between similar-looking individuals, while the "lumpers" stress the similarities. A great example of this is the Mormon Metalmark (*Apodemia mormo*), a Western U.S. species. Some authorities see this as a single species with several subspecies, whereas others view at least some of the subspecies as separate species. Different populations of Mormon Metalmarks fly at different times, are geographically separate, and/or have different caterpillar host plants. With time, these subpopulations will likely evolve into different species or die out as their environment changes. Therefore, whether they are lumped into one species or split into several species is somewhat arbitrary.

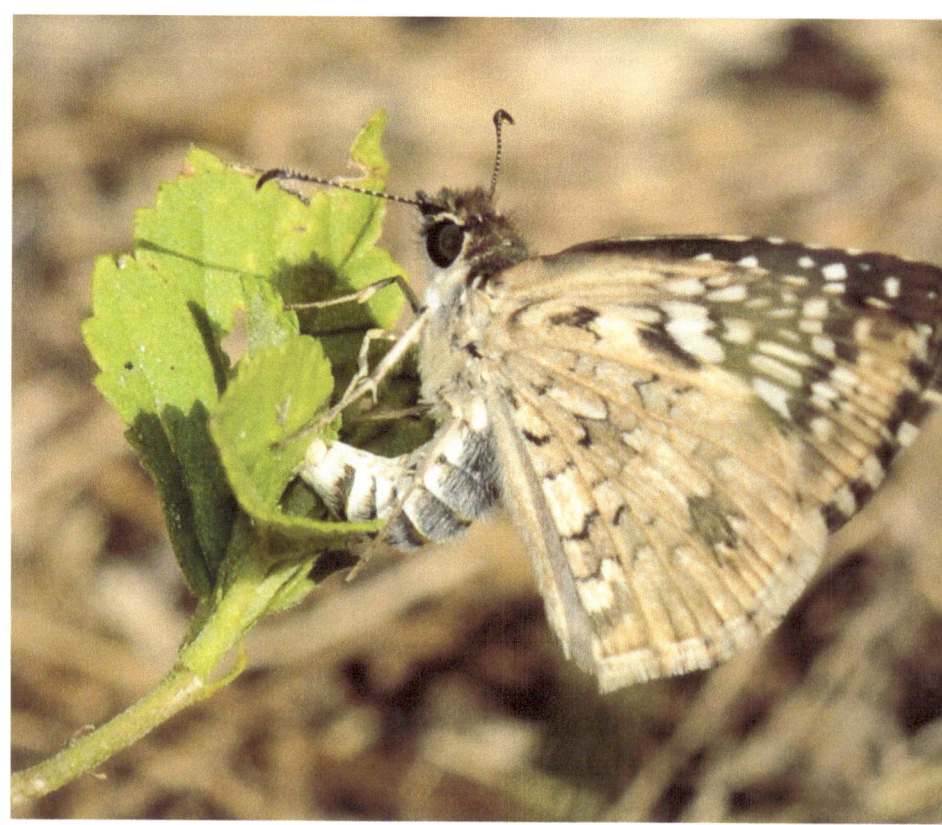

A Tropical Checkered Skipper (*Pyrgus oileus*) ovipositing on *Sida sp.* (a member of the Mallow family), its host plant. The egg is visible as a white sphere at the tip of the butterfly's abdomen. Photo taken at Eco Pond, Flamingo, Florida (Everglades National Park), Nikon D300 with 180 mm lens, ISO 640, F11, 1/1000 sec.

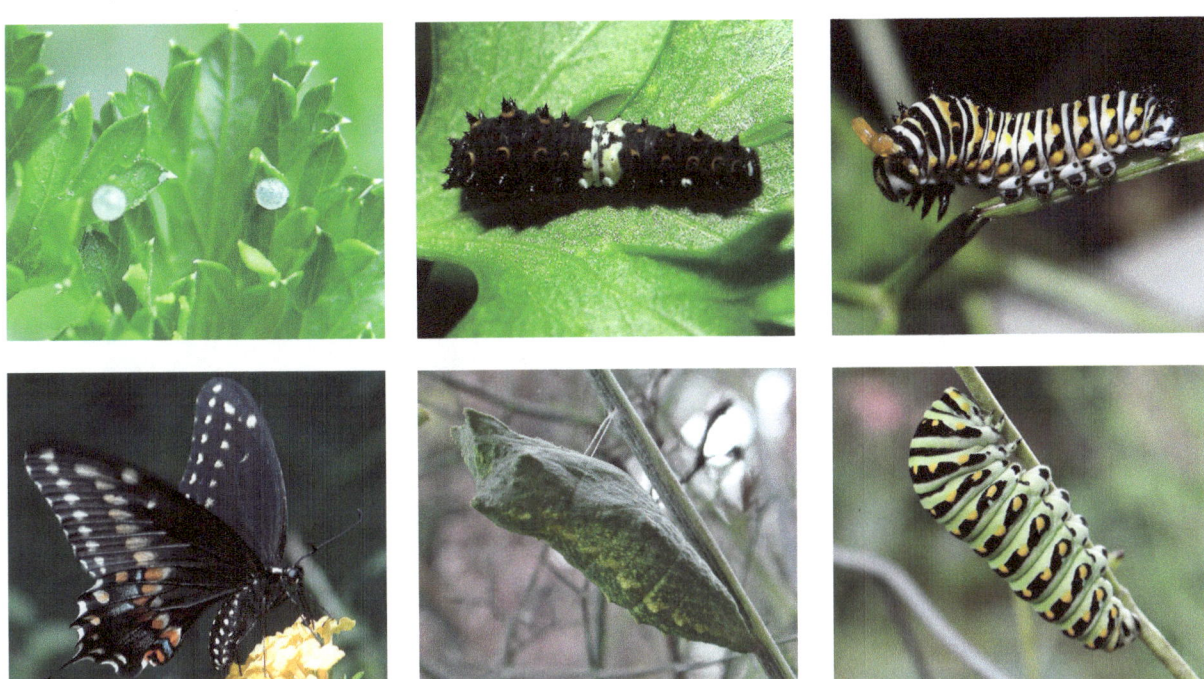

Black Swallowtail lifecycle: clockwise from upper left – eggs on parsley, early instar caterpillar, middle instar caterpillar, caterpillar about to form chrysalis, chrysalis, adult. All photos taken in Durham, North Carolina, with Nikon Coolpix 8700 camera.

Butterflies start life as an egg laid on a host plant. Each butterfly has a plant or a group of related plants that serves as the host plant for its caterpillar. Monarchs only lay eggs on milkweeds; Black Swallowtails use members of the Parsley family; Pipevine Swallowtails lay eggs on Pipevines, etc. The female butterflies sense their host plants through chemical receptors on their antennae and legs. It is not unusual to see butterflies hopping from plant to plant in search of their host plant. A female butterfly typically alights on a host plant, curls its abdomen beneath it, and extrudes a sticky egg onto a leaf or flower.

After usually a week or less the egg hatches into a tiny caterpillar. The caterpillar immediately starts eating, and although some eat only at night to avoid predators, most eat continuously. As a caterpillar grows, it must shed its outer skin (exoskeleton). It does this four times, more or less, with each stage being called an instar. Instars, even of the same species, can look different from each other.

After the caterpillar reaches a sufficient size, or exhausts its food supply, it forms a chrysalis (pupa). To do this, the caterpillar often leaves its host plant, looking for a safe place to hide. In most cases, the caterpillar initially forms a "J" shape, in which it hangs upside down from an attachment to a twig, and which may last for up to a day or more. Then, often over the course of several minutes, the caterpillar sheds its exoskeleton for the last time to reveal a chrysalis underneath. Inside the chrysalis the caterpillar is metamorphosing into an adult butterfly, a process which can be as short as 1-2 weeks, or as long as a season or more. (Butterflies may overwinter as eggs, caterpillars, chrysalises or adults, although each species does it in only one way). As the chrysalis approaches maturation, it often changes color, and may reveal the colors of the adult butterfly within. Finally, the chrysalis splits open, the adult crawls out, pumps blood into its wings to inflate them, and once the wings dry, it flies off to look for a mate and nourishment.

Baltimore Checkerspot (*Euphydryas phaeton*) caterpillars feeding on a Turtlehead (*Chelone glabra*) leaf in July. Often they are encased in a web, but here web fibers are barely visible. The small black dots are frass (feces). Each caterpillar is less than ¼ inch long. Photo taken in Camden, Maine, Nikon D300 camera with 60 mm macro lens, ISO 400, F10, 1/160 sec.

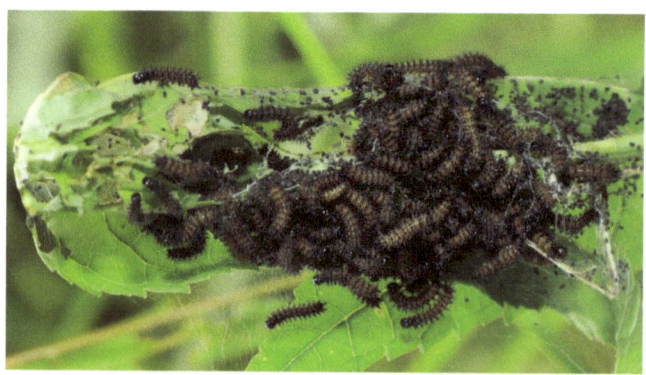

Baltimore Checkerspot caterpillar, fifth and final instar, feeding on Arrowwood (*Viburnum dentatum*) in May. Because of predation, the number of caterpillars is usually reduced greatly, and they are no longer colonial. Photo taken in Stockton Springs, Maine, Nikon D300 camera, 180 mm macro lens, ISO 400, F5, 1/500 sec.

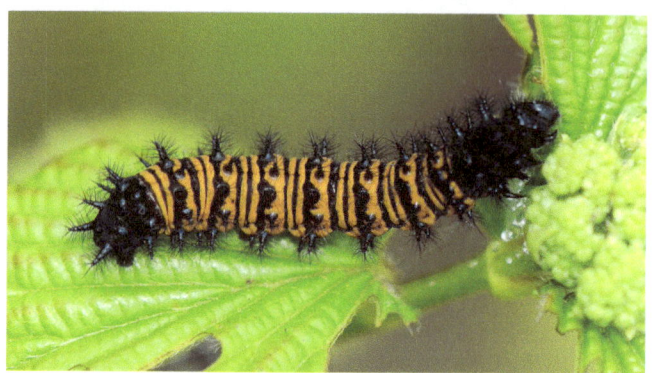

Adult Baltimore Checkerspot in June, taken about 3 weeks after the previous photograph in the same location. Nikon D300, ISO 400, F11, 1/500 sec, no fill flash. An exposure compensation of -0.3 F stops was used to help prevent the large amount of black on the butterfly from causing the photo to be overexposed (see Page 50).

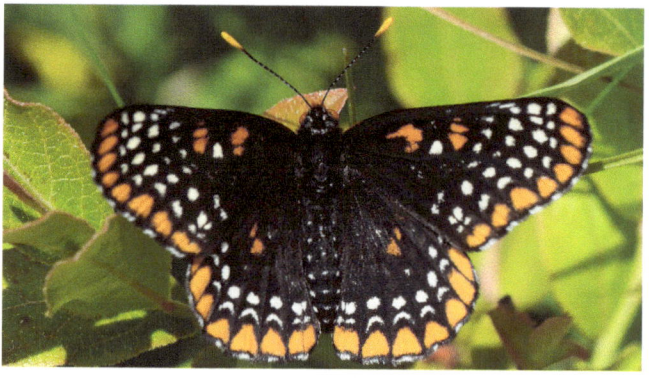

Because the main purpose of the adult butterfly is to reproduce, they usually only live three weeks or less. Exceptions include butterflies that overwinter as adults or migratory butterflies, such as the Monarch, which goes through 3-4 generations each summer before the last generation in North America flies south in the fall to roosting colonies in California or Mexico. The following spring they fly north and resume the reproductive cycle. An excellent website for viewing videos of the various stages of butterfly maturation is the Butterflies of Singapore website (http://www.butterflycircle.com) and blog (http://butterflycircle.blogspot.com). The website contains thousands of excellent butterfly photos and videos.

Each butterfly is a specialist to varying degrees. Some butterflies, such as the Cabbage White or Orange Sulphur, can be found throughout much of North America, whereas others are much more restricted, often due to availability of their host plant, suitable nectar plants, temperature extremes or other environmental conditions. Moreover, many butterflies are only found at a specific time of year in any given location. Therefore, if one wants to photograph a particular butterfly, or its caterpillar, knowledge of the butterfly's natural history is often essential. Such knowledge, however, may not be enough. There are dramatic year-to-year variations in butterfly abundance and in the abundance of individual species. Each species is part of a large ecological web, and its population is influenced by known and unknown factors such as extremes in weather and abundance of predators. For example, many species are expanding their range northward, most likely as a result of global warming.

One example to illustrate the complexity of butterfly natural history is the Baltimore Checkerspot. This is an Eastern North American butterfly that is only found in moist meadows that contain its host plant, turtlehead (*Chelone glabra*). The adult flies in late June to early July, laying eggs on turtlehead. The eggs hatch in July. The caterpillars are colonial feeders (staying in groups), usually going through three instars before they cease feeding. Initially they go into a resting phase inside a colonial web. Then,

in the fall, they descend to the ground to hibernate for the winter. In the spring they resume feeding, but are no longer as particular in what they eat. Once they reach sufficient maturation (5th instar), they form a chrysalis and emerge as a butterfly.

While most butterflies are attracted to nectar-bearing flowers, the preferences of different species may vary according to size, shape, color and odor of flowers. Some butterflies prefer tree sap or rotting fruit as a food source. Some can also be found slurping liquid from wet spots on the ground, presumably as a source of minerals. When one sees such activity, and carefully approaches the butterflies, occasionally they can be induced to crawl up on your finger, by placing your finger just in front of the butterfly.

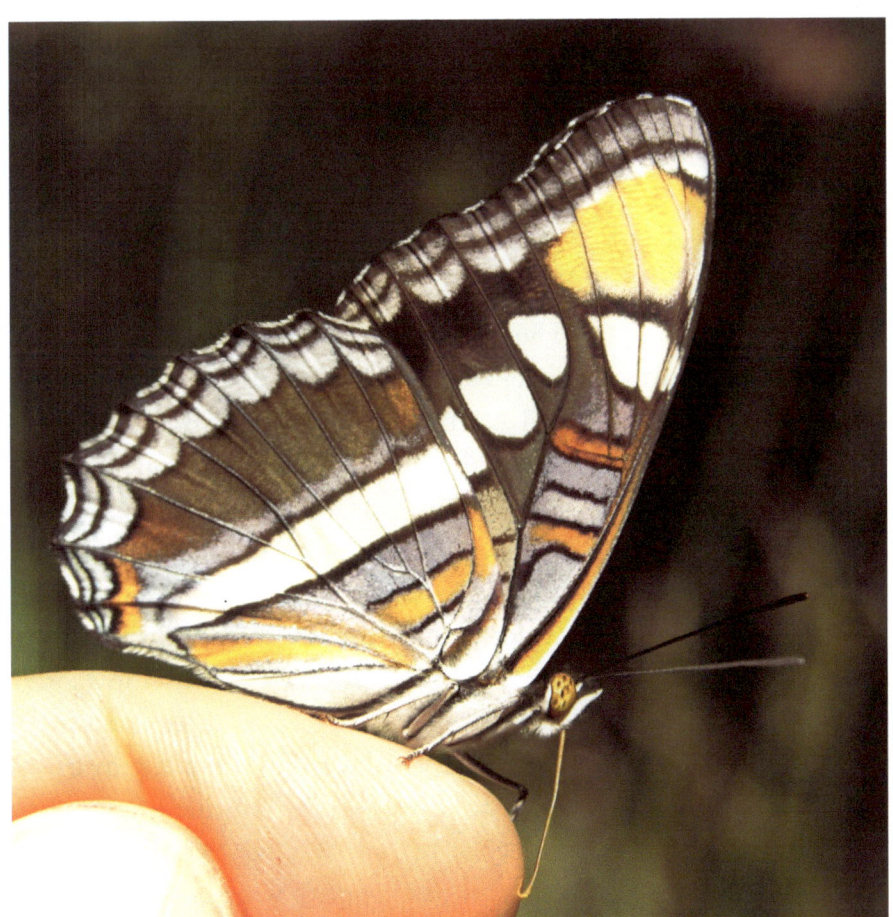

Arizona Sister (*Adelpha bredowii*) sipping sweat from a finger. This butterfly is often hard to approach, as it flies high above the ground. However, when "puddling" on dirt or gravel, it can be readily approached. Photo taken in Ramsey Canyon, Arizona. Nikon Coolpix 8700 camera, ISO 50, F4.6, 1/210 sec.

Cabbage White (*Pieris rapae*) using its proboscis to slurp nectar from a Goldenrod flower. Photo taken in Camden, Maine. Nikon D300 camera, ISO 400, F11, 1/400 sec.

Butterflies imbibe liquids through their proboscis, a long tube that is curled up when not in use. Although all butterflies have a proboscis, its length and other aspects of a butterfly's anatomy seem to determine which nectar plants an individual species prefers.

How to Find Butterflies

The single best way to learn about butterflies in any given location is to locate a local butterfly club and join their butterfly walks. The North American Butterfly Association (NABA; www. naba.org) has local chapters, and even if none are in your area, NABA is often a good way to find the contact information for knowledgeable butterfly enthusiasts near you. Alternatively, many butterfliers are also birders, and local Audubon Society Chapters will often know people who do both. The two hobbies are complementary. Bird activity dies down as the day warms up, just around the time that butterflies become active. It is difficult to do both at the same time; birders look up, and butterfliers look down.

The best days for butterfly photography are warm, sunny days with little or no wind. Butterfly activity decreases greatly if clouds block the sun. And it's much easier to get sharp photographs when the butterflies and flowers are not buffeted by the wind.

Butterflies usually fly from the first warm days in the spring to the last warm days in the fall. Butterflies that are single brooded, however, usually have a period of only a few weeks when the adults fly in any given location. In order to see all the butterflies in an area, one will need to revisit that location from early spring through the fall. Some butterflies are found only near water, others prefer open fields and others seek the shade of forests. My first recommendation, however, is a negative: avoid areas where pesticides are used. Over the past decade, I have visited the Florida Keys repeatedly, trying to re-experience the large variety of butterflies I saw on my initial trip. Each subsequent trip the number and variety of butterflies have decreased. I suspect that this is due to widespread insecticide use to suppress mosquitoes. My last visit was just before the 2012 elections, and there were even road signs for people running for the local mosquito control board. I doubt their motivation was an interest in preserving biodiversity. I am probably one of the few people who see the presence of mosquitos as a positive!

Certain habitats are hotspots for butterfly photography. The first is the presence of nectar sources (flowers). Although one can photograph a butterfly on a leaf, twig, dirt or pavement, the most compelling photographs are usually taken with butterflies on flowers. Therefore, one of the best places to look for butterflies is fields, especially where the field abuts a forest, river or pond. In many parts of North America fields are not natural, but must be maintained through periodic cutting. In this regard, power lines can be great places to look for butterflies, as long

as pesticides and/or herbicides have not been used recently. Similarly, agricultural fields usually suffer from the use of pesticides. However, the edges of an organic farmer's field or roadside borders can be great places to find wildflowers, butterflies, and other insects. Mountain meadows are wonderful places for wildflowers and butterflies, as long as one visits during the relatively short wildflower season. Some species congregate on hilltops, while others prefer wet environments.

Other great spots for butterflies are botanical gardens, parks and, of course, butterfly houses. Many botanical gardens and some parks now have their own butterfly gardens. Not only are they a great place to see butterflies, but the staff can often provide helpful advice on what plants

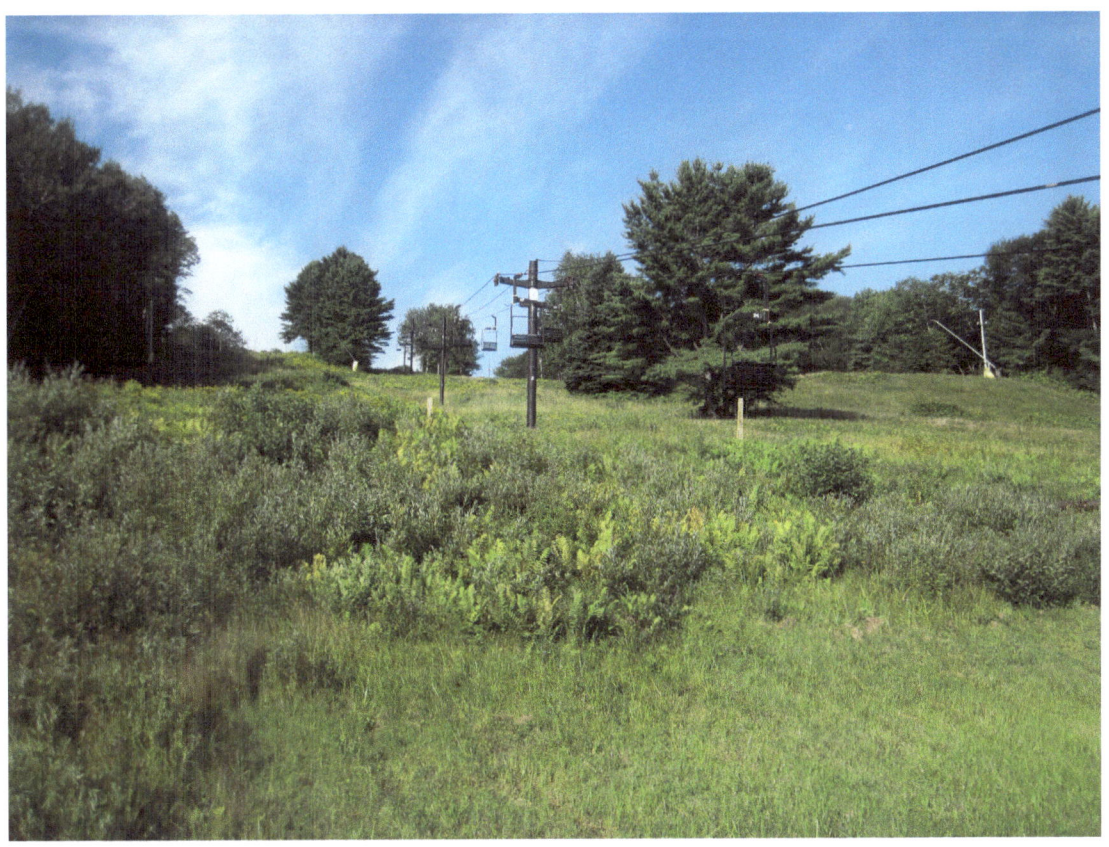

Camden (Maine) Snow Bowl. Ski slopes should not be overlooked, and are excellent spots to look for butterflies. They are kept open by mowing, usually only once a year in the fall, are surrounded by forest, and have a great variety of microhabitats, including those of species that are mainly found above treeline.

to use to establish your own butterfly garden. Butterfly houses often purchase chrysalises of non-native species, many of which are tropical in origin. They also have lots of nectar plants, so it's easy to photograph exotic butterflies in association with attractive flowers. The one negative is that there are often many people visiting butterfly houses, including young children, so the noise and activity level can be high, precluding a peaceful experience.

When I travel in North America, I usually use the North American Butterfly Association website (www.naba.org) to meet local butterfliers or, at least, find out where good locations are. While there are many butterfly hotspots in North America, an outstanding place to see

and photograph butterflies is the National Butterfly Center in Mission, Texas (http://www.nationalbutterflycenter.org). The Center has a large array of gardens to attract butterflies and is located in one of the top spots for butterfly diversity in North America. When traveling abroad, which I used to do often for work, I use www.birdingpal.org to find local birders who often know great spots to see both birds and butterflies.

Attracting Butterflies

A great way to photograph butterflies is to establish your own butterfly garden. The key ingredients are a sunny area, ideally protected from the wind, with a combination of nectar

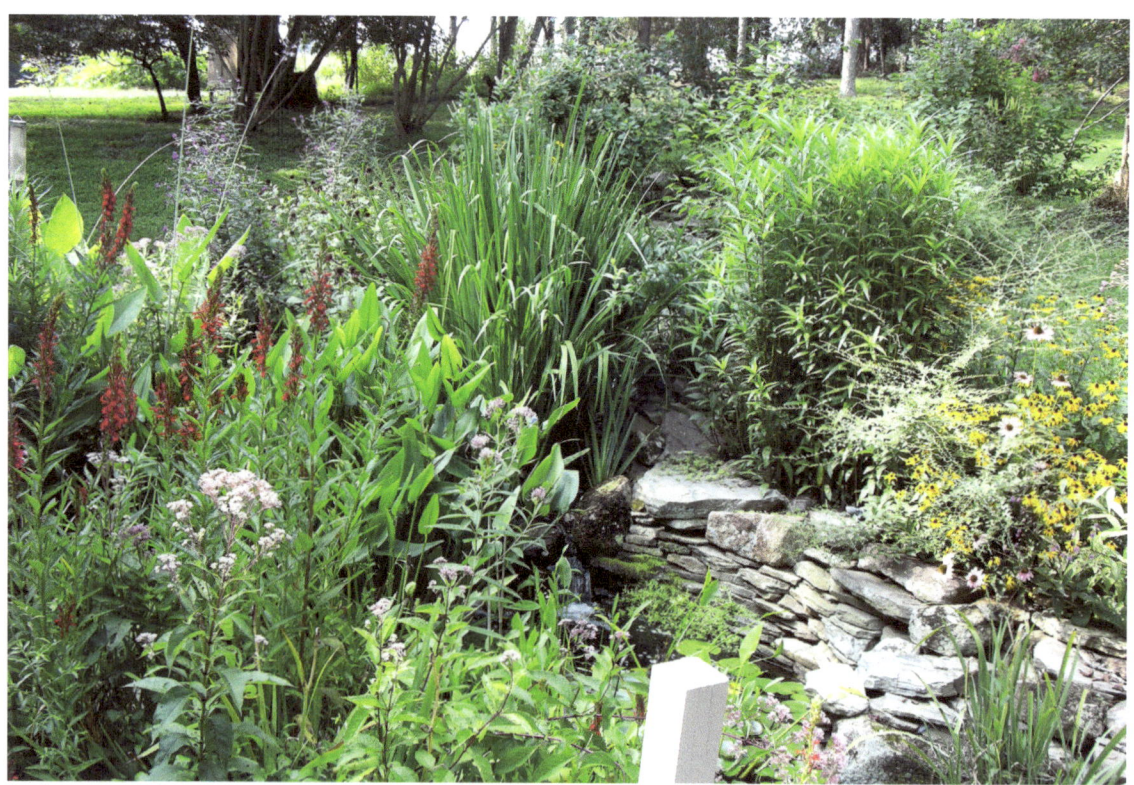

Part of the author's butterfly and water garden in Durham, North Carolina. Some key plants (not all visible) are Asters (*Symphyotrichum species*) , Bergamots (*Monarda sp.*), Butterfly Bushes (*Buddleia sp.*), Cardinal Flower (*Lobelia cardinalis*), Coneflower (*Rudbeckia sp.*), Giant Hyssop (*Agastache sp.*) Goldenrods (*Solindago sp.*), Joe Pye-weed (*Eupatorium sp.*), Lantana, Milkweeds (*Asclepias sp.*), New York Ironweed (*Vernonia noveboracensis*), Sunflowers (*Helianthus sp.*) and Zinnias. If the garden appears a bit out-of-control, it was. In pots on a porch away from the garden were Tropical Milkweeds (*Asclepias curassavica* – host plant for Monarchs) and Parsley (*Petroselinum crispum* – host plant for Black Swallowtails).

plants and host plants, wet sand or fine gravel for butterflies that like to obtain minerals from dirt, and a piece or two of ripe fruit for butterflies that are attracted to sap. It helps to know what butterflies are likely to be found in your area, when they fly, and what type of flowers they visit. The nectar plants should include a variety of plants that bloom from early spring into the late fall (or all year around if the weather permits). As far as nectar plants are concerned, a good source of information is a local plant nursery. There are also several good websites:

- North American Butterfly Association has many regional butterfly gardening guides for the United States (http://www.nababutterfly.com/guide_index.html).

- The University of Minnesota extension service offers a general guide on butterfly gardening (http://www.extension.umn.edu/distribution/horticulture/DG6711.html).

- The University of Texas at Austin maintains a list of native plant species for each area of the United States (http://www.wildflower.org/collections/), as well as species that attract butterflies (http://www.wildflower.org/collections/collection.php?collection=bamona).

- Will Cook, an avid naturalist and butterfly photographer, has useful tips for butterfly gardening in North Carolina, much of which is applicable throughout the Eastern United States (http://www.carolinanature.com/plants4leps.html).

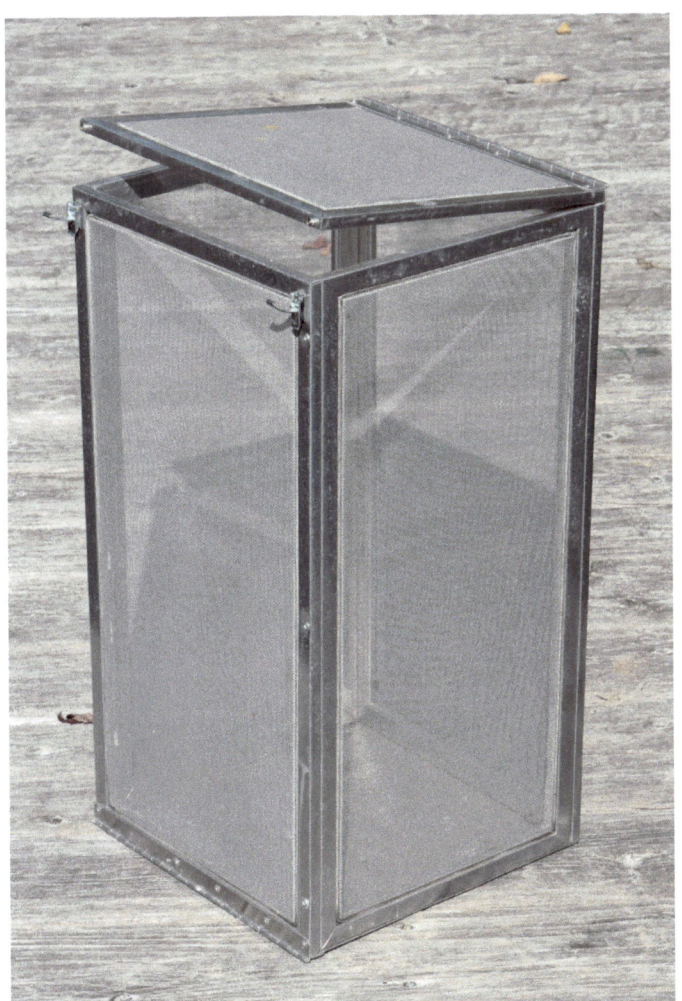

This screened enclosure is ideal for rearing butterfly eggs or caterpillars through to adults. The eggs or caterpillars can be placed on a potted host plant, protecting them from predators. Alternatively, the cage can be placed over a plant in the field. Similar cages can be easily made using wood and screening. For other ideas, search the Web under "insect rearing cages".

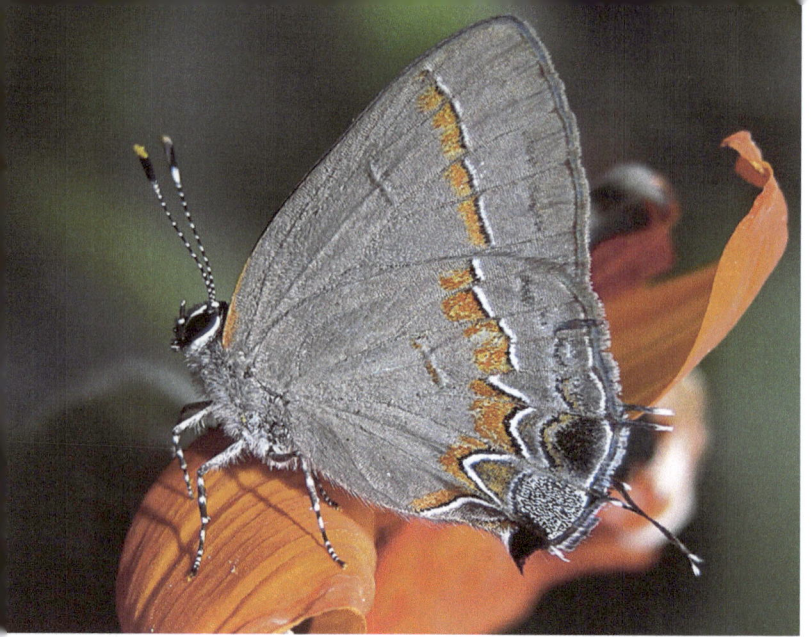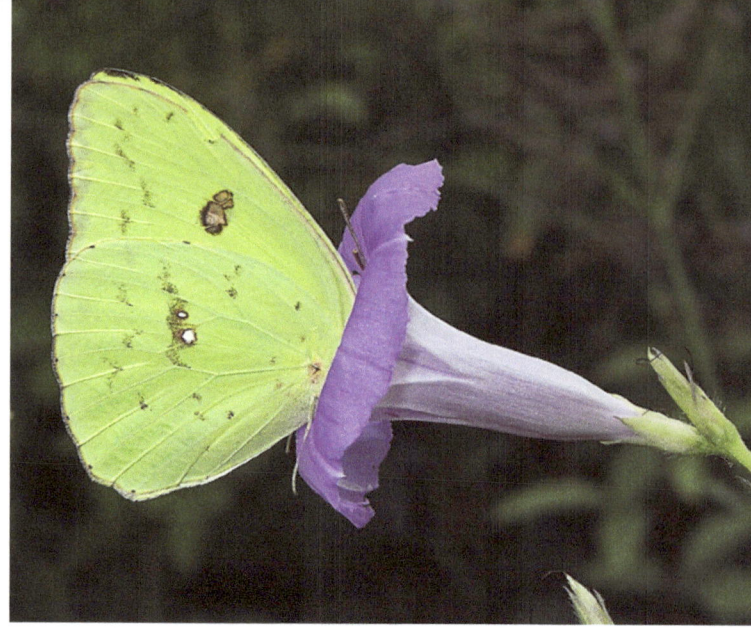

By choosing flowers that are dramatic or complement a color on the butterfly, the beauty of the butterfly is enhanced. Left: Red-banded Hairstreak (*Calycopis cecrops*) on Mexican Sunflower (*Tithonia diversifolia*). Right: Cloudless Sulphur (*Phoebis sennae*) on a Morning Glory. Both photos taken with a Nikon Coolpix 8700 camera. Left: ISO 50, F 3.5, 1/250 sec. Right: ISO 100, F 4.7; 1/250 sec.

When planning your butterfly garden, if possible, it is best to separate caterpillar host plants from nectar plants. Nectar plants attract not only butterflies, but many other insects, some of which prey on caterpillars. In order to improve caterpillar survival, one can transplant caterpillars and leaves/branches of the host plants into a protective, screened enclosure and raise them until adulthood.

Once you learn what butterflies frequent your yard and their habits, it is worth planting flowers that will not only attract a particular butterfly, but will complement the butterfly's colors. A little advanced planning can heighten the chance of getting the best image. Some of my favorite flowers are zinnias, because they come in a large variety of sizes and colors. They can make even dull butterflies look spectacular. It is also wise to plant at least some flowers that are not easily blown about by the wind.

Developing an Eye for Butterflies

Novice butterfliers are often amazed at the number and variety of small species that they never realized were butterflies, including skippers, blues, metalmarks, elfins and hairstreaks. It takes practice to spot these small butterflies; however, this skill can be rapidly acquired. Walking slowly, scanning the flowers and brush, the astute observer will look for discontinuity in color, shape or motion. Pretty soon, you'll be able to differentiate the flight of a bee, wasp or fly from that of a butterfly or moth. Separating butterflies from day-flying moths can be a bit more difficult. Butterflies are often more colorful, have a more erratic flight, and often land with their wings together. Moths usually land with their wings flattened against a leaf or the ground. If you get a good look at the antennae, moths almost always have straight or pointed antennae (sometimes feathered), whereas butterflies have a thickening, club or hook at the end of the antennae, at least part of which is a different color or pattern from the rest of the antennae.

A pair of close-focusing binoculars greatly aids the search and identification of butterflies. In general they should be 7x or 8x (the degree of magnification), focus down to about 5 feet or less, and have large enough lenses to see well in low light. A good overview of close focusing

Which is the moth and which is the butterfly? The insect on the right has antennae with a fine, tapered end, whereas the one on the left has a club on the end of its antennae.

American Copper (*Lycaena phlaeas*)

Faithful Beauty (*Composia fidelissima*)

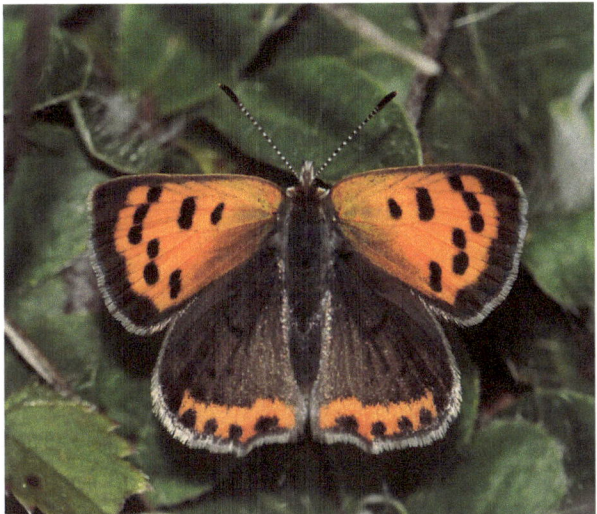
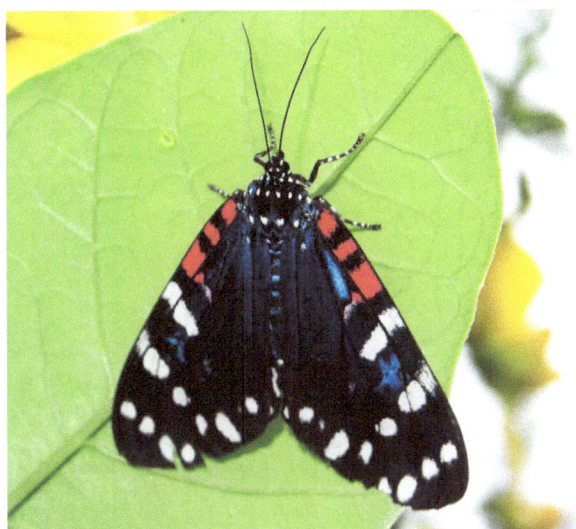

binoculars can be found at http://www.naba.org/binocs.html.

How to Identify Butterflies

Photographers have an advantage over other butterfly watchers: they can record what they see for future reference and study. While some butterflies, such as the Swallowtails, can be identified quickly with the naked eye, others require the use of binoculars to see the necessary detail. Still others are best identified by careful examination of photographs. The western Greater Fritillaries (*Speyeria* spp.) are a case in point. Differences between some species are slight, and the variability within a given spe-

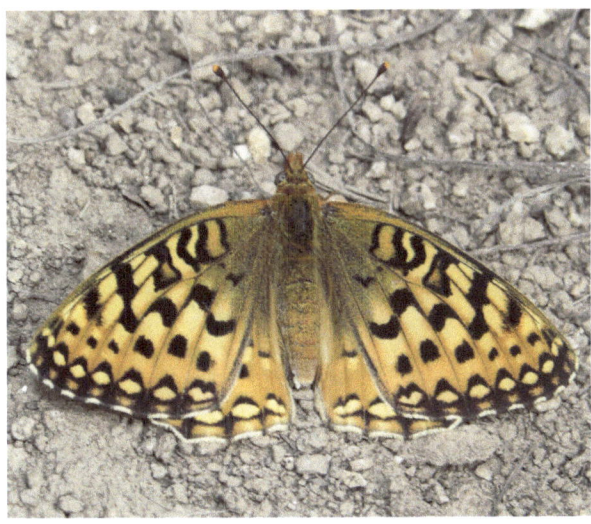
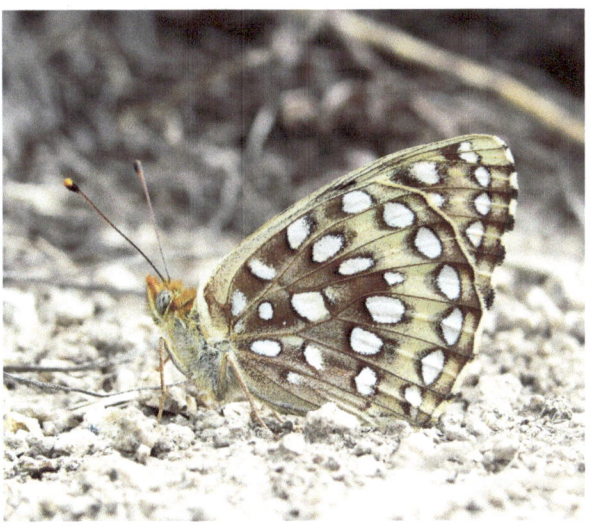

These photographs were taken of one of the greater fritillaries in mid-July in a mountain valley in Alta, Utah. Based on the photographs, time of year and location, this is likely to be either a Zerene or Coronis Fritillary (*Speyeria zerene* or *Speyeria coronis*). Coronis is usually larger, but the relative size is not possible to assess from the photographs. When I posted images of this butterfly on BugGuide (www.bugguide.net), it led to an interesting discussion of the possible subspecies of greater fritillaries present in Alta (http://bugguide.net/node/view/739499). Photos taken with Nikon Coolpix 8700 camera, ISO 50, F4.5, 1/180 sec (left photo), 1/70 sec (right photo).

cies is large. Photographs of both the upper and lower surface of the wing are often needed for identification, along with knowledge of the location, habitat and time of year. Without photographs or collecting the butterfly, identification of a western Greater Fritillary may be impossible.

When viewing and photographing butterflies, it is important to take note of its overall size, and the color and pattern of both the upper and lower wing surfaces (if possible). For some spe-

cies the presence and location of spots and/or bars is important.

It is helpful if you can narrow the insect to one of the six butterfly families: Swallowtails (*Papilionidae*); Whites, Sulphurs and Yellows (*Pieridae*); Blues, Coppers and Hairstreaks (*Lycaenidae*); Metalmarks (*Riodinidae*); Brushfoots (*Nymphalidae*); and Skippers (*Hesperiidae*). Even if you are uncertain, by comparing your specimen to photos in one of the field guides, the identification usually is obvious. Because it

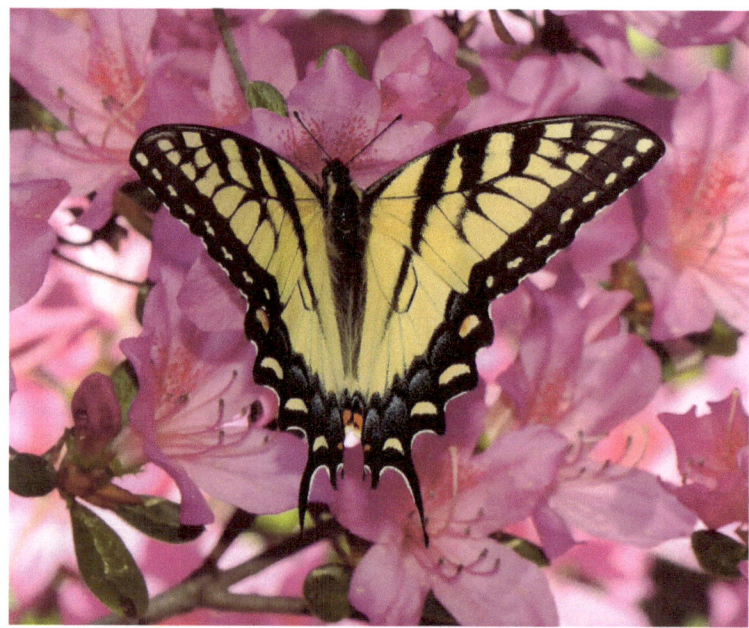

Eastern Tiger Swallowtail (*Papilio glaucus*). **Swallowtails** are large butterflies with a predominantly yellow or black color. Most have "tails" on their hindwings, reminiscent of the tails of barn swallows, hence the name "swallowtail". Photo taken in Durham, NC. Nikon D300 camera, ISO 800, F13, 1/320 sec.

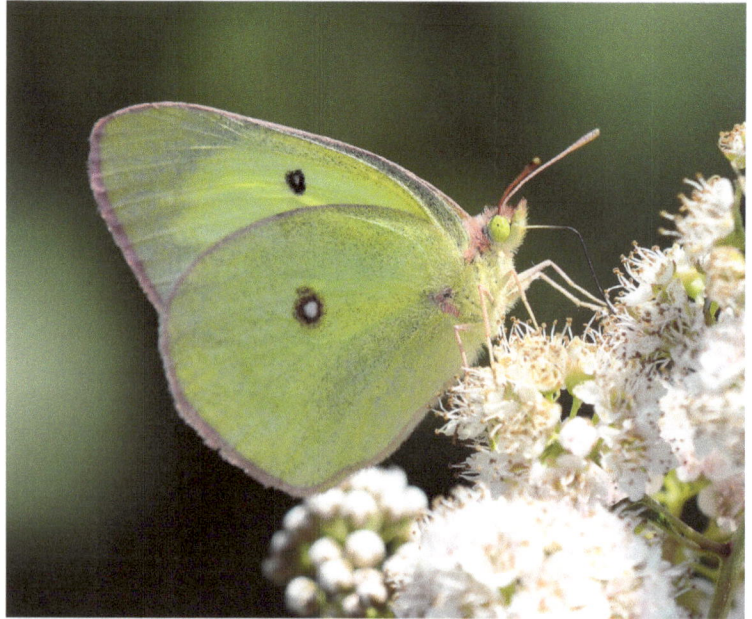

Pink-edged Sulphur (*Colias interior*). **Whites, Sulphurs and Yellows** have the distinctive colors suggested by their names. They range from small to large in size, often land with their wings closed, and tend to spend little time on any one flower. Photo taken near Petit Manan National Wildlife Refuge, Steuben, Maine. Nikon D300 camera, ISO 400, F 8, 1/800 sec.

is difficult to remember the minor differences between closely-related species, the task is much easier if you have a photographic record of what you saw.

There are many butterfly field guides and the number increases each year. Some general ones useful in North America include Jeffrey Glassberg's Swift Guide to Butterflies of North America or his Butterflies through Binoculars series (Eastern North America, Western North America and Florida) and Jim Brock and Kenn

Blues, Coppers (not shown) **and Hairstreaks** are small butterflies that often have brightly colored spots and/or bars on their wings, often on the trailing edges. It is thought that these markings serve to distract predators, thereby lessening the chance that a predator will strike at the butterfly's head or body. Left photo taken near Sierra Vista, Arizona, Nikon D300 camera, ISO 250, F 6.3, 1/500 sec. Right photo taken near Tucson, Arizona, Nikon D300 camera, ISO 500, F11, 1/1250 sec.

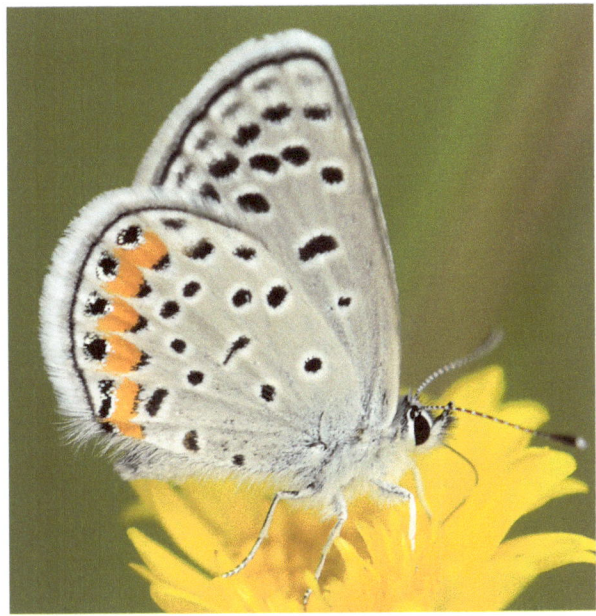

Acmon Blue (*Plebejus acmon*)

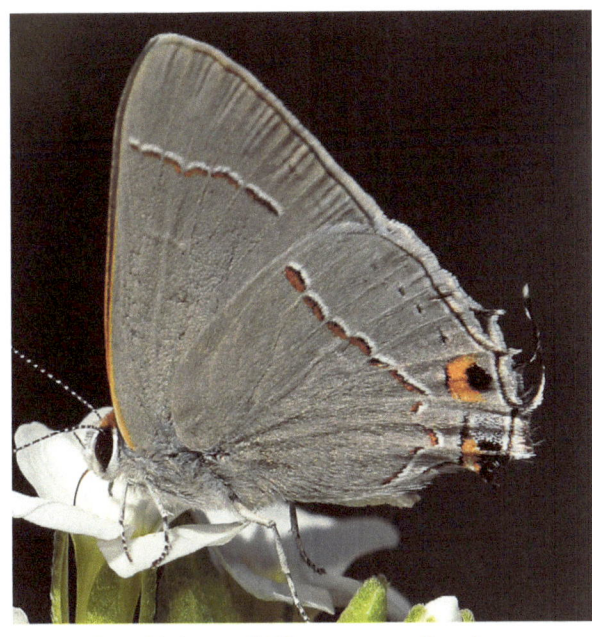

Gray Hairstreak (*Strymon melinus*)

Red-bordered Metalmark (*Caria ino*). **Metalmarks** are generally small orange and black butterflies with varying amounts of white, metallic markings, giving them their name. They usually land with their wings open. Photo taken in Bentsen-Rio Grande Valley State Park, Mission, Texas. Nikon Coolpix 8700, ISO 50, F4.4, 1/120 sec.

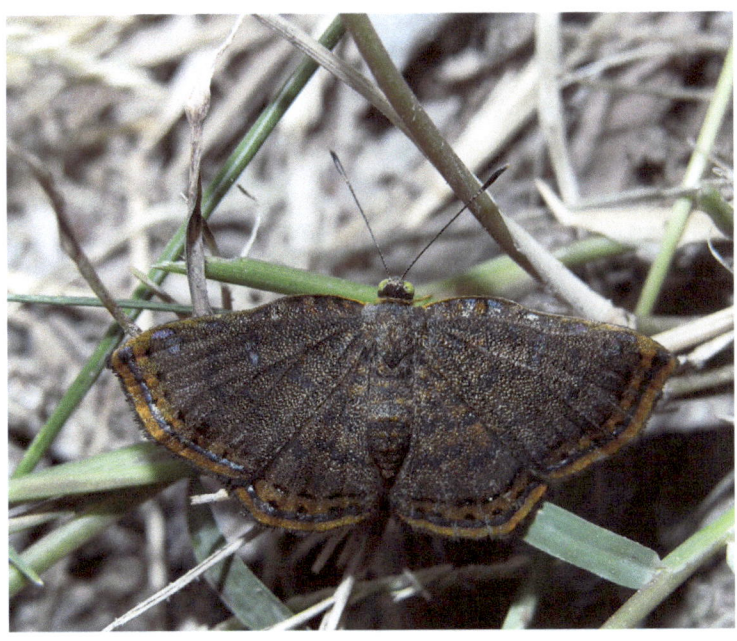

Gulf Fritillary (Agraulis vanillae)   Painted Lady (*Vanessa cardui*)

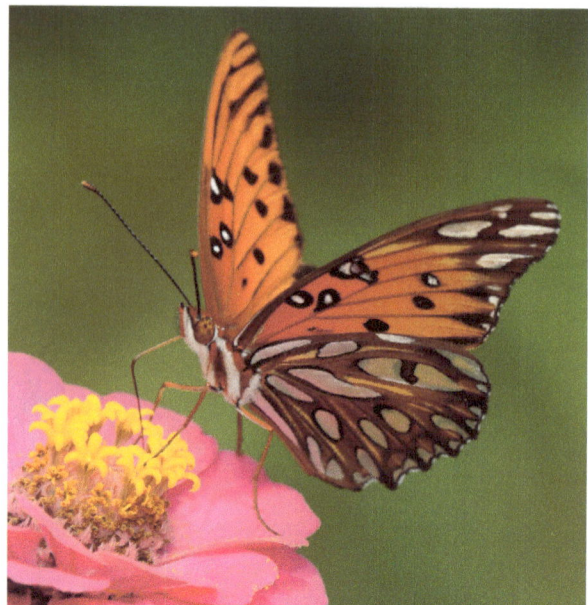
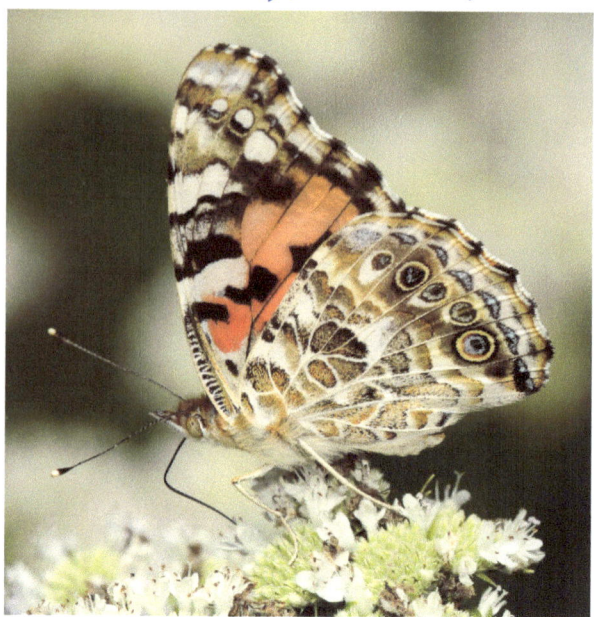

The best way to think about **Brush-footed butterflies** is that they are the butterflies that are not in one of the above four families and are not skippers. They are characterized by markedly reduced and hairy front legs (hence the name), legs that are often difficult to see in the field or in photographs. These forelegs are attached just behind the eyes. Brushfoots vary in size, shape and color, defying any unifying description. If you see a butterfly that appears to have only four legs, it is likely a brushfoot. Left photo taken in Beaufort, North Carolina. Nikon D300 camera, ISO 400, F10, 1/320 sec. Right photo taken in Lincolnville, Maine, ISO 200, F10, 1/800 sec.

Skippers make up about a third of all butterfly species in North America. They are often confused with moths by novice butterfliers, and some may be difficult to identify to species. Skippers have antennae that are bent at the ends, but this can be difficult to see. Spread-wing skippers often land with their wings flat (left photo). Grass skippers, the most common kind, either land with their wings together (right photo) or with their hindwings flat and the forewings raised about 45 degrees. Left photo taken near Tucson, Arizona, Nikon D300, ISO 400, F11, 1/500 sec. Right photo taken in Craven County, North Carolina, Nikon Coolpix 8700, ISO 50, F4, 1/160 sec.

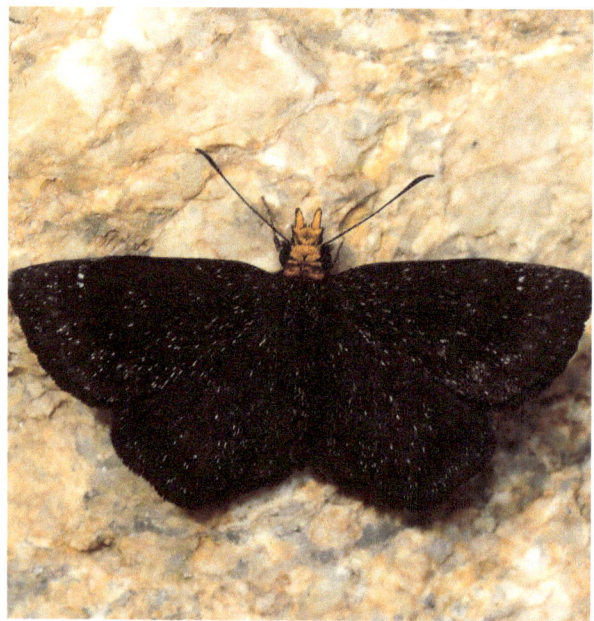
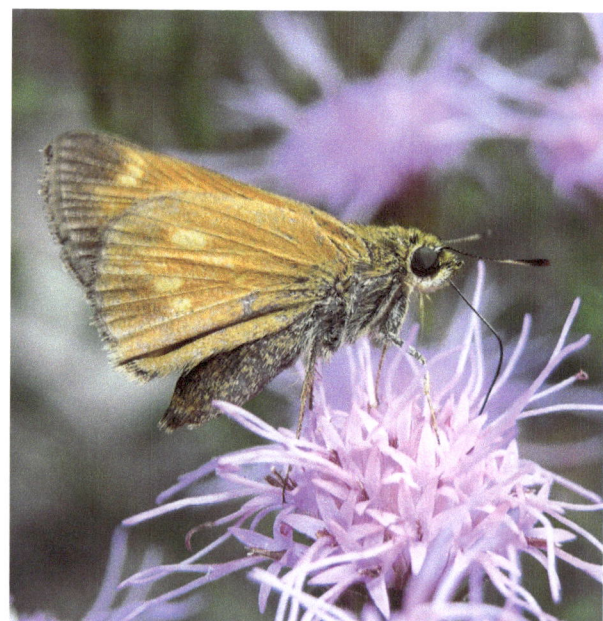

Golden-headed Scallopwing (*Staphylus ceos*)   Yehl Skipper (*Poanes yehl*)

Kaufman's Butterflies of North America. For those who prefer smart phones, Audubon Field Guides has a Butterfly App. The App works best to confirm a presumptive identification; it is not easy to scroll quickly through a long series of butterflies.

If you are uncertain about the identification of a butterfly, an excellent way to identify it is to post a photograph on the web. One website for identifying unknown insects, including butterflies, is BugGuide.net (http://bugguide.net/), a volunteer-driven catalog of North American (United States and Canada) bugs, started around 2004. After registering, which is free, you can upload the photograph of an unknown specimen, and often within minutes to a few hours, someone will tell you the identity of your bug. Alternatively, you can search the photos on BugGuide that others have submitted for a match to the butterfly photo you have taken. I find this easier to do with a field guide, but the advantage of BugGuide is that there are likely to be many photos of a butterfly, showing the variability that can occur in a species. Often, there will also be photos of the caterpillars and chrysalises of that species. In addition, by using the "Data" link in BugGuide, one can quickly see where and the time of year a particular species has been photographed in your area.

Another site to submit images of unknown butterflies is Butterflies and Moths of North America (http://www.butterfliesandmoths.org). As the name implies, this site includes both butterflies and moths. It not only contains excellent photos of preserved and live butterflies, caterpillars and chrysalises of many species, but also provides information about the natural history of the butterflies, including their ranges.

A third site is Butterflies of America (http://butterfliesofamerica.com/), which has excellent photographs of butterflies throughout North, Central and South America. For the United States and Canada, it shows examples of color variation within a species, as well as the various subspecies of a butterfly. It does not currently have a mechanism for submitting unknown butterflies, but if you think you know the butterfly, it is a good place to go for confirmation.

Neotropical Butterflies (http://www.neotropical butterflies.com) is a site specializing in butterflies of the New World tropics. It provides an easy means of quickly scanning a large number of thumbnails, once you've narrowed an unknown specimen to a particular family of butterflies.

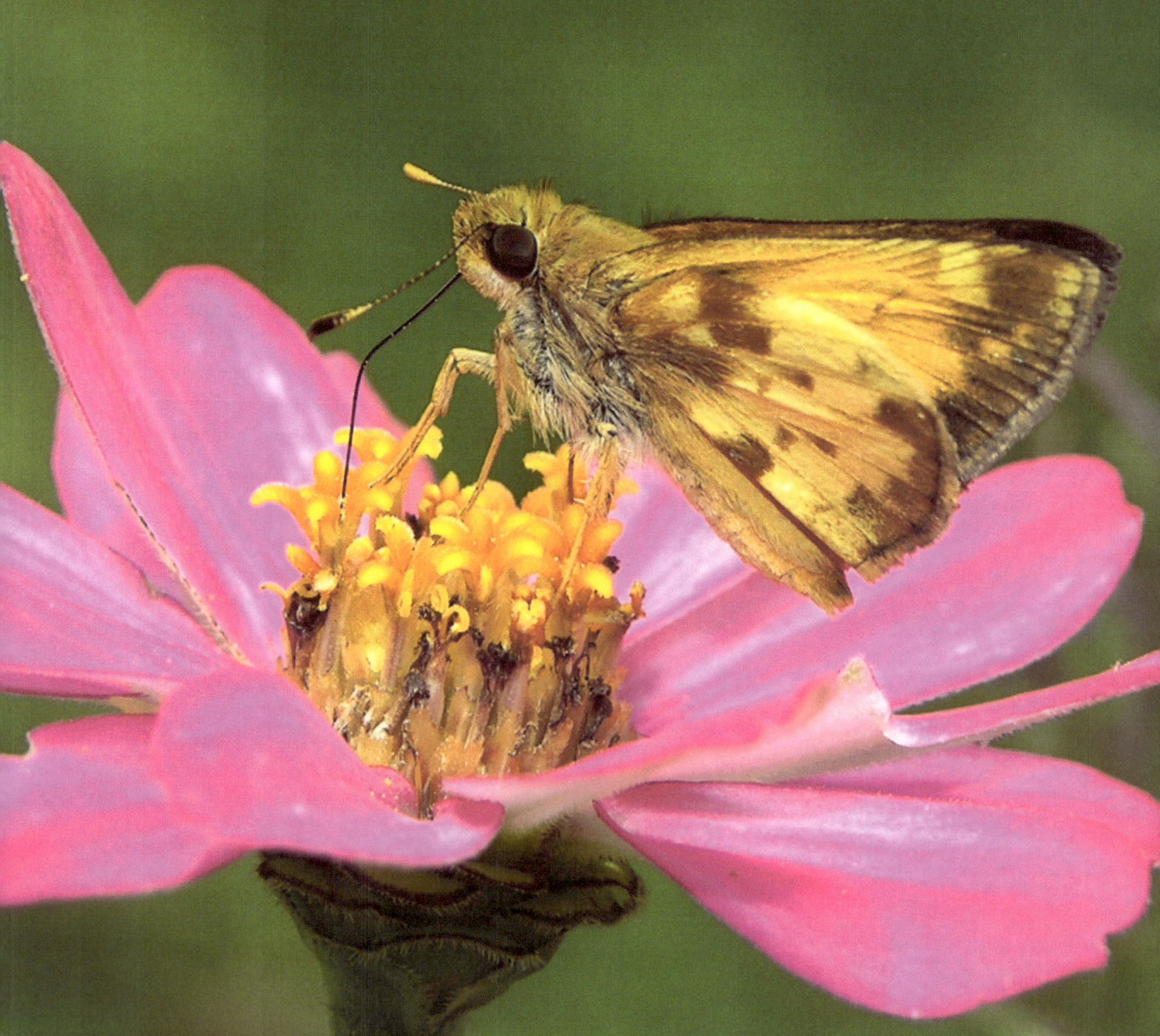

Section 2
Photographic Equipment

Introduction

Although butterfly photography can be challenging, the advent of digital photography greatly speeds up the learning curve. One has rapid feedback on the quality of an image, and the incremental cost of taking 100 or 1000 pictures in a day is insignificant. Butterfly photography requires equipment that can produce sharp images, with accurate exposure and color rendition. In choosing photographic equipment, one needs to consider the camera, the lens and the flash.

In researching photographic equipment, there are several excellent websites, and many more blogs and ad hoc opinions and explanations from outstanding photographers. The websites I visit most frequently in this regard are Digital Photography Review (www.dpreview.com), Steve's Digicams (www.steves-digicams.com), and Ken Rockwell's site (www.kenrockwell.com). Another strategy is to put your question into a search engine to access the myriad opinions on almost anything photographic. In this section I will cover only the highlights of photographic equipment as it relates to butterfly photography, and encourage the reader to use the in depth information available on the web.

There are two basic approaches to digital butterfly photography equipment with lots of variations. The first is to use a close-focusing, point-and-shoot (P&S) camera. The second is to use a digital single-lens reflex (DSLR) camera with a macro lens. Each has its advantages and disadvantages, and sometimes I carry both in the field. Because new camera models come out every year, I will focus on key features of camera systems, rather than specific models.

Point-and-Shoot Cameras

Overview

The naming of camera types is a bit confusing. The name "Point-and-Shoot" (P&S) is really a misnomer in the context of butterfly photography, because the high quality models necessary for good butterfly photography are anything but simple. They are also called compact cameras, but this term makes them easy to confuse with compact digital single lens reflex (DSLR) cameras, described starting on Page 31. High-end P&S cameras are also called "bridge cameras", to connote the sense that they have features of both P&S and DSLR cameras. P&S (including bridge) cameras are characterized by a built-in lens and the absence of the mirror that is present in SLR cameras. Because there is no mirror, the viewfinder views the scene through a different lens from the one being used to acquire the image. All P&S cameras also have a liquid crystal display (LCD) screen, which does provide an electronic image of the subject, using information provided by the sensor.

Using the LCD screen

The biggest advantage of a P&S camera is the ability to get close, really close (down to 2 cm). Outstanding sharpness can be obtained by combining close focusing with the high quality lens in top-of-the line P&S models. Of course, getting close to a butterfly is challenging even without a camera, and if you try to look through the viewfinder, your body heat, breath and shadow will scare the butterfly away. One way to circumvent this problem is to use the LCD screen at arm's length to compose the photo. This requires a steady hand, but the lightness of P&S cameras, with or without image stabilization (vibration reduction) technology, makes this approach feasible. One disad-

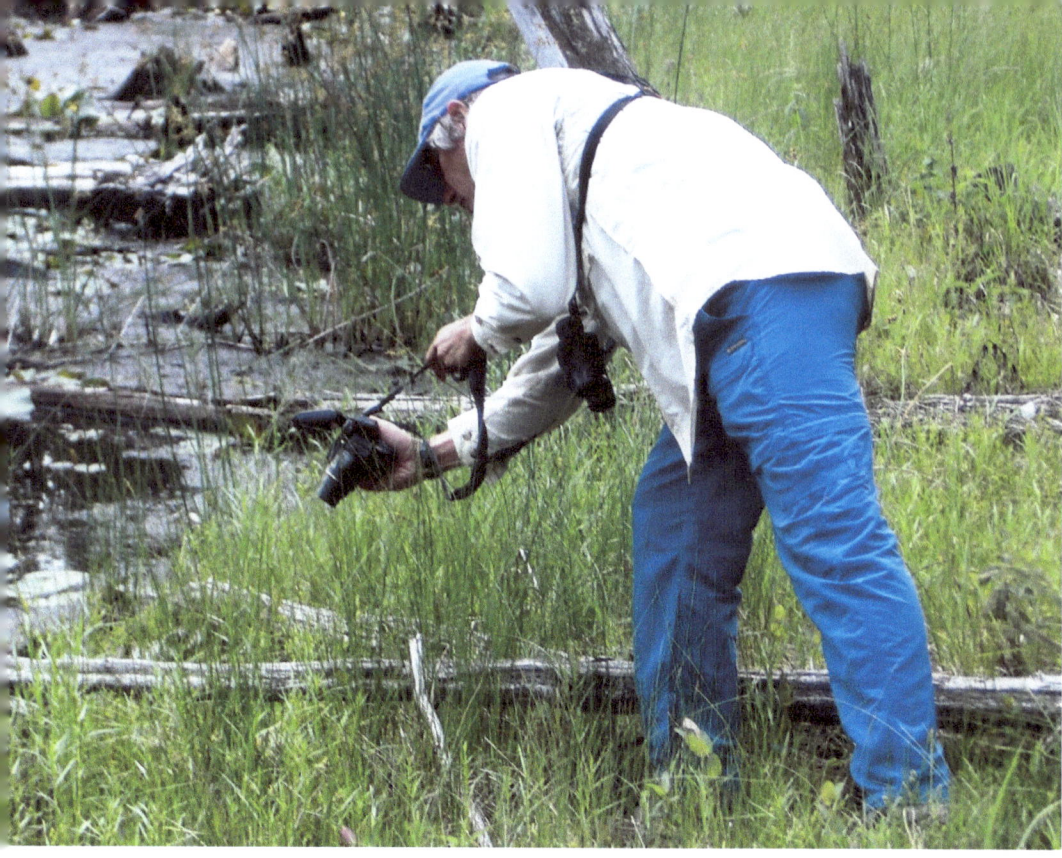

The author using the LCD screen on a point-and-shoot camera to compose the image with the camera held at arm's length. (Photograph courtesy of Donald J. Tindall)

vantage of using the LCD screen as a viewfinder is that it uses up batteries much quicker than using the viewfinder itself.

Another important feature to look for is an articulating ("flip-out and twist") LCD screen, and not simply a flip-out screen. This means that the LCD screen can pivot away from the camera allowing the photographer to choose the angle at which to photograph the subject. This is a big advantage in butterfly photography. If the butterfly's wings are not facing you, simply rotate the camera parallel to the wings, rather than trying to change where you are standing. If a butterfly is near the ground, no problem, simply rotate the LCD screen so that

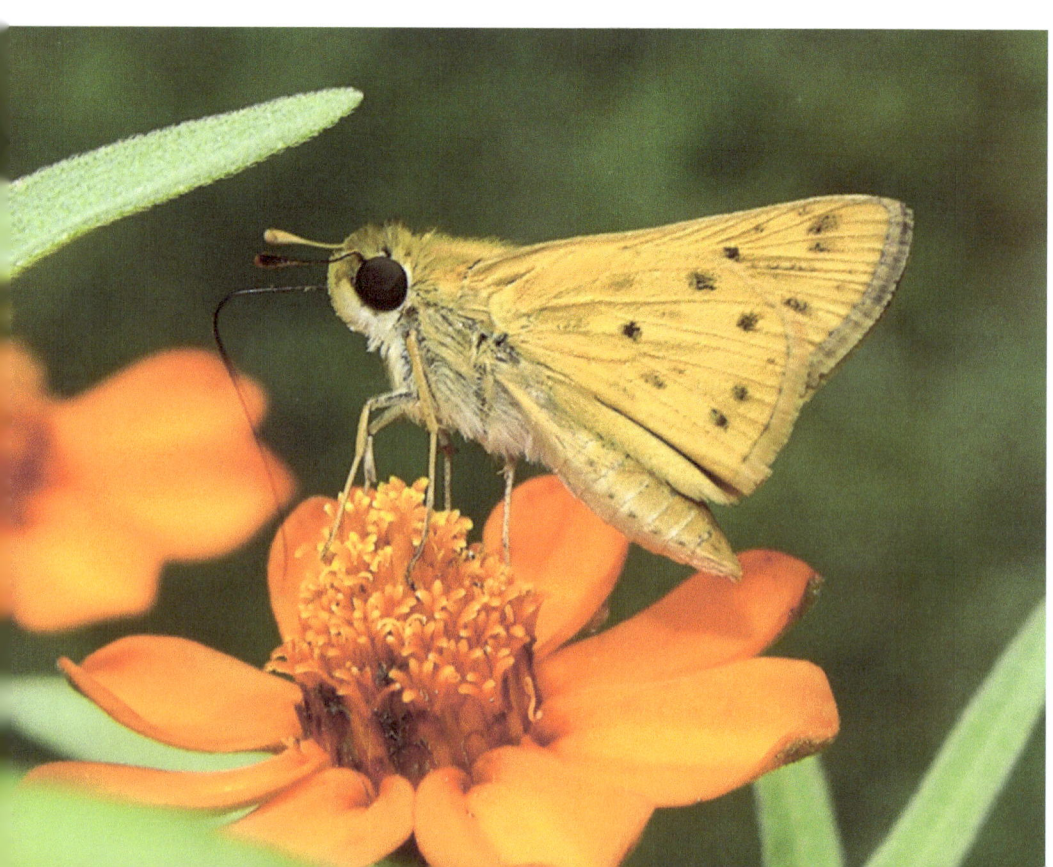

This Fiery Skipper (*Hylephila phyleus*) was "skipping" among flowers in a patch of Zinnias. Because of the denseness of the vegetation, this photo was facilitated by placing the point-and-shoot camera (Nikon Coolpix 8700) close to the butterfly among the leaves and using the LCD screen to compose the image. ISO 50, F4.8, 1/175 sec.

you are viewing the image looking down, with the camera near or on the ground. One can really appreciate this feature in southern climates, where chiggers and ticks abound! Although LCD screens have improved greatly in recent years, the image can still be difficult to see in bright sunlight.

Lenses

Because the lenses on P&S cameras are an integral part of the camera and cannot be changed, they will be discussed here. You'll want to get the camera with the best close-up lens possible, as this will be the single most important feature for outstanding butterfly photography. Many butterflies are small, and to take the best photos of them with a P&S camera, you'll need to get close. The quality of a lens is determined mostly by the quality of the glass used inside the lens and the coatings applied to the glass to reduce flare and ghost images. Another important attribute is the light-gathering capacity with wider lens being brighter. This is referred to as the maximum aperture (lens opening) with the

smaller "F" numbers being wider. Avoid P&S cameras with long telephoto lens. These lenses require more glass, are not as sharp, and have smaller effective apertures, especially at the longer focal lengths. The only place I see a long telephoto lens being useful on a P&S camera is to capture an image of a distant butterfly for identification purposes, but the image will often be clearer using a shorter focal length and enlarging the photo on a computer.

Flashes

I normally use a fill flash (more on flashes on Pages 36-39), but the built-in flash of most P&S cameras is useless with close-up photography. The lens tends to get in the way of the flash, and the photograph is usually overexposed because the flash power cannot be reduced sufficiently. One has a choice of not using a flash or having a separate flash mounted on a hot-shoe. Not using a flash is OK in bright sunlight, but not in partial or full shade, and even in bright sunlight the image will generally look better with a fill flash. Only high end P&S cameras have

A point-and-shoot camera showing many of the key features for butterfly photography:
- High quality, medium telephoto lens capable of focusing down to about two inches
- Hot shoe for external flash
- Low power external flash
- Articulating LCD screen

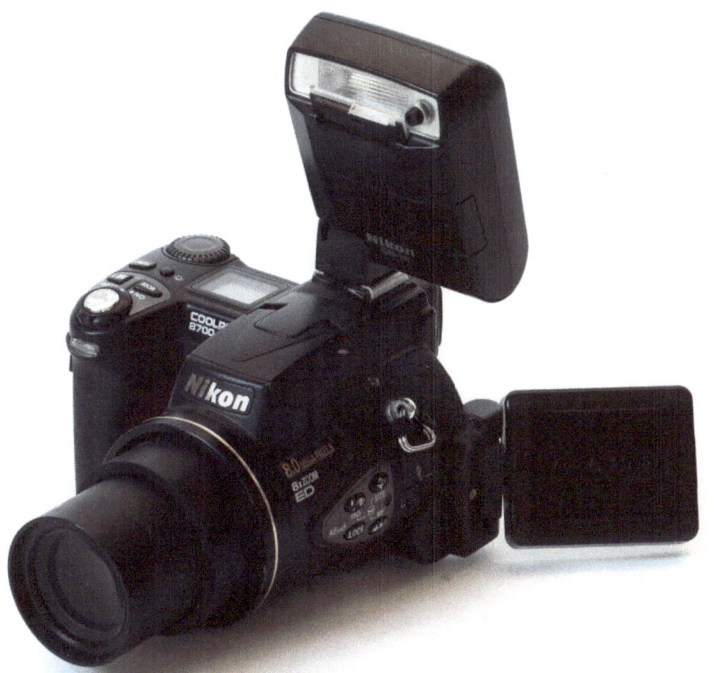

Nikon Coolpix 8700 camera with a Nikon SB-30 flash

a hot shoe, which is essential for close-up flash photography of butterflies. With P&S camera flashes, the smaller the flash, the better. The Nikon SB-30 flash shown on the previous page is entirely manual, but it doesn't take long to learn empirically how much flash is needed in a given situation. The flash has a built-in diffuser, which is essential at the close camera-to-subject distances inherent in photographing butterflies with a P&S camera.

Other features

A few high-end P&S cameras now have vibration reduction, a useful plus in butterfly photography. This allows photographs to be taken at slower shutter speeds to improve light-gathering ability, or alternatively, at a higher F-stop to increase depth-of-field.

Another feature to look for on P&S cameras is the speed of image processing (the rapidity with which photos can be taken). Perhaps the greatest frustration with P&S cameras is watching a butterfly fly away or change orientation in the time it takes the camera to focus or prepare for the next shot.

A word about "megapixels": avoid paying more for more megapixels in a P&S camera. All high end P&S cameras made today have an ample number of pixels in their sensors for most uses (12 megapixels or more). The size of the sensor is important, and the larger sensors in DSLR cameras will have a greater number of pixels and allow greater detail in the photo. P&S cameras use small sensors, and squeezing more pixels into these sensors means each pixel is smaller. This translates into lower light sensitivity and, potentially, more noise (see next paragraph). The image quality also depends on the quality of the lens and sensor, as well as the number of pixels.

The sensitivity of the sensor to light is called the ISO value: the higher the ISO value, the less light that will be needed for any given image. The ISO can be adjusted in all cameras, but the greater the ISO value, the more likely the image quality will deteriorate due to noise and graininess. One can think of ISO as the signal to noise ratio; at high ISO values and low light there is a low signal to noise ratio, and one is likely to see increased graininess and minute white dots or discoloration in the photo. The greater the enlargement of the image, the more likely one is to notice the noise. Noise is also more apparent in shadows or in low light, especially if the images are lightened using image processing software.

All images have some noise, and many cameras have noise reduction software that is incorporated into the formation of a JPEG file. This is why a RAW file can look grainier than the JPEG derived from that RAW file. Because most butterfly photographs are taken in bright light, noise is generally not a major problem,

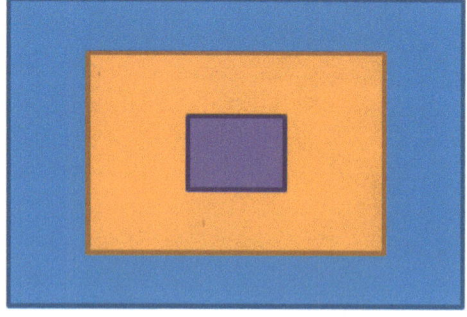

Comparison of relative sensor sizes: A typical point-and-shoot camera uses a 7.6 x 5.7 mm sensor shown in purple. A typical compact DSLR uses a 23.5 x 16.6 mm sensor shown in orange. A full-frame DSLR uses a 36 x 24 mm sensor shown in blue.

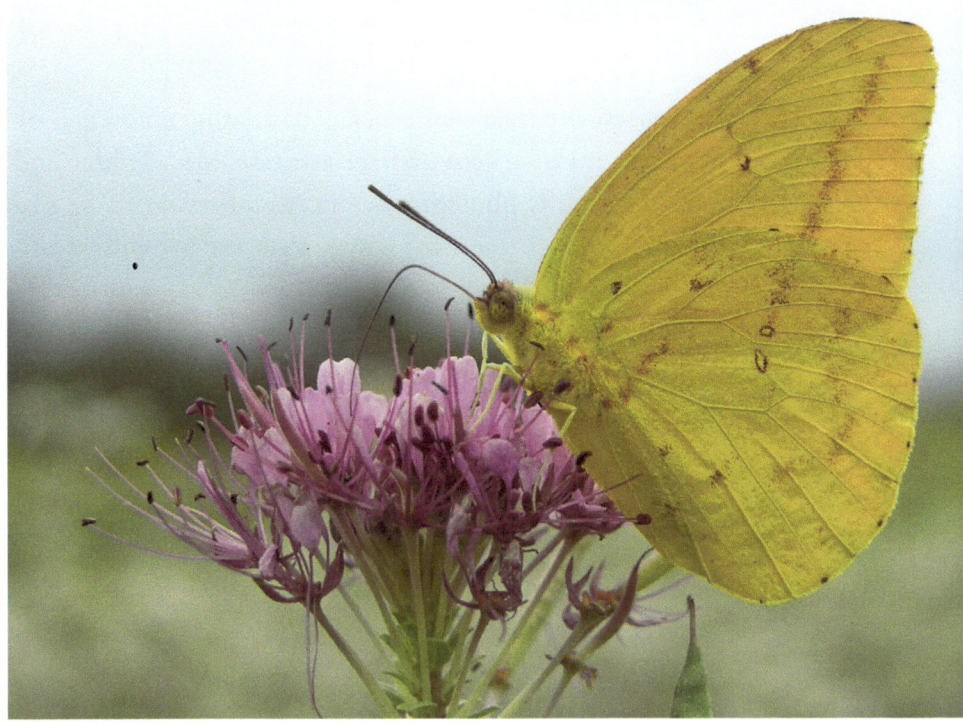

This photo of a Large Orange Sulphur (*Phoebis agarithe*) illustrates the challenge of blurring the background with a P&S camera. The photo was taken at ISO 50, F3.5, 1/600 sec. Although the butterfly and flower stand out against the distant background, I would have preferred a featureless background. Photo taken in the Rio Grande Valley, Texas.

and increasing the ISO is a good way to allow for greater shutter speeds. The ISO range on P&S cameras is limited to lower values, because of the lower light gathering capacity of the small sensors. In general, P&S cameras can function adequately at ISO values up to 200-400. Although cameras may be advertised as having much higher ISO values, the quality of the image will suffer, and one should not pay more for a camera, solely because of the presence of higher ISOs.

Disadvantages of P&S cameras

There are several important disadvantages to P&S camera. First of all, the small image sensor on P&S cameras means that there are fewer pixels available to record the photograph. For close-up photography, this limitation is overcome by being close, but in the telephoto range, image quality is noticeably reduced and light-gathering ability goes down substantially. Secondly, the autofocus systems on most P&S cameras are slow compared to those on DSLR cameras, causing a delay between when the shutter release is pressed and the image taken. This can be frustrating when trying to capture an image of a hairstreak twisting and twirling on a flower or a

butterfly opening and closing its wings. Thirdly, the LCD screen does not provide as clear an image as the viewfinder on an SLR camera. Because of the above limitations, many photo opportunities will be missed. Also, the lenses used on P&S cameras, with their greater depth-of-field, make it harder to achieve the pleasing blurred backgrounds achievable with telephoto macro lens. This can be partially overcome by placing a one or two diopter close-up filter in front of the lens. This requires that the lens is threaded in order to accept filters. The filter will not only blur the background, but will prevent the camera from focusing on the background, rather than the subject. However, it also limits the cameras ability to focus on distant objects and reduces the depth of field. The greater the diopter number, the more the background will be blurred, and the greater the limitation to focusing on distant subjects.

Finally, many lenses on P&S cameras have external focusing, meaning that the lens telescopes in and out as it focuses. There is nothing inherently wrong with this focus system, but it is easy for fine dirt or sand to get inside the moving parts of the lens. Nevertheless, the comparatively low cost, improved clarity by being close to the subject, and the benefits of an articulating LCD screen make a P&S camera a reasonable option for butterfly photography. Bottom line: if you choose to go the P&S route, look for a camera with a high quality, close-focusing lens, vibration reduction, a hot shoe for an external flash and an articulating LCD screen. Other attributes that are useful are a fast autofocus and minimal delay between pressing the shutter release and the photo being taken, although neither of these features are strengths of P&S cameras. These cameras are constantly improving and capable of producing excellent photos.

Mirrorless cameras

Some of the shortcomings of P&S cameras are being overcome by a new class of camera: the mirrorless cameras. These are true "bridge" cameras. Like P&S cameras, they do not have a mirror. But like DSLRs, they usually have large sensors and interchangeable lenses. The absence of a mirror means the camera can be lighter and quieter than a DSLR, and the lens can be placed closer to the sensor. Combined with a large sensor, the resulting image quality can match or exceed that of a DSLR equipped with a comparable lens. Because there is no mirror, the cameras cannot have an optical viewfinder that views through the lens. Instead, the viewfinder, if one exists, must be digital, meaning that there is a small LCD screen inside the viewfinder, as well as the large LCD screen on the back of the camera. The attributes one would want in a mirrorless camera are the same as those for a P&S camera. One drawback is a limited choice of lenses, and in most cases the autofocus mechanism is slow. On some of the cameras, a traditional SLR lens can be attached to the camera using an adapter, but this tends to make the autofocus mechanism even slower, if it works at all. To date, only one model has a fully articulating LCD screen. Most of these limitations can be overcome, and already mirrorless

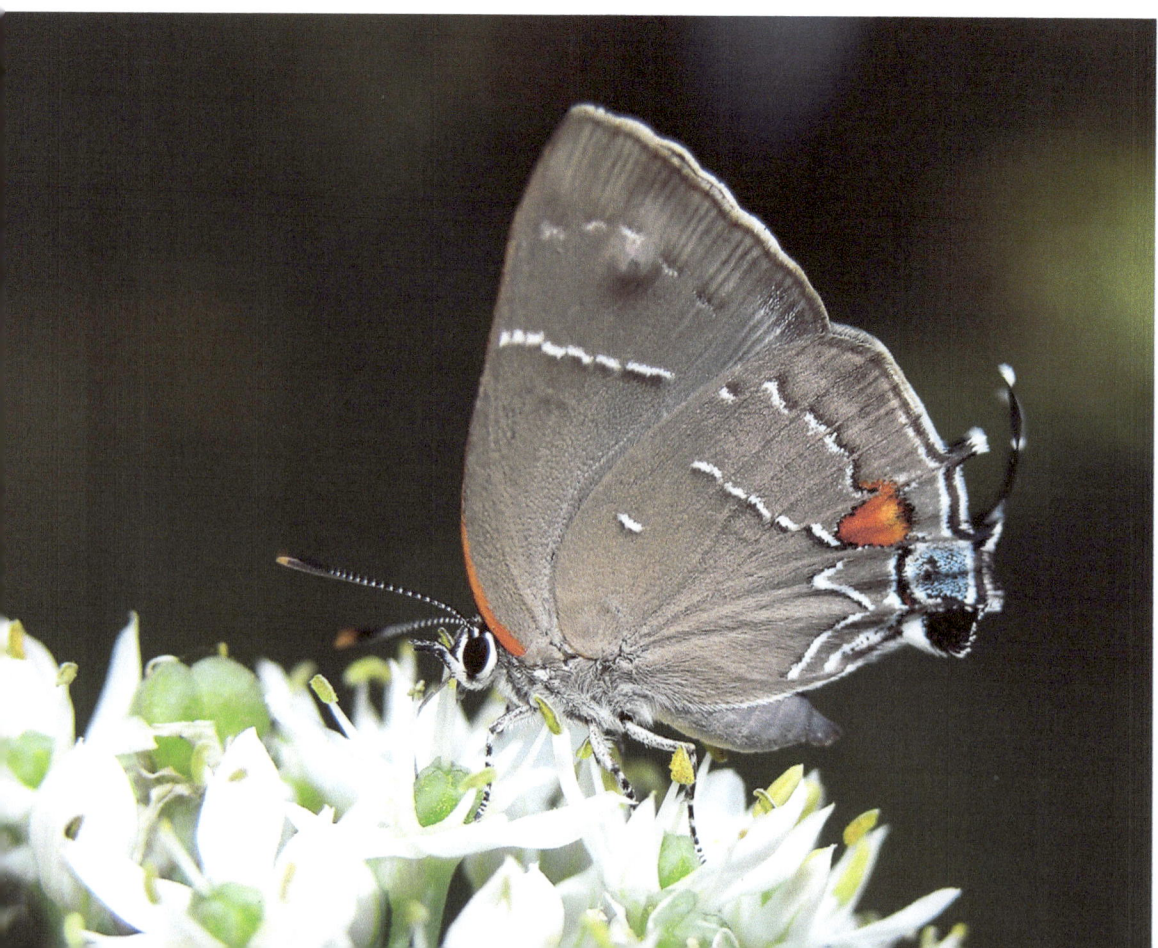

This image of a White-M Hairstreak (*Parrhasius m-album*) illustrates the importance of having a lens with excellent sharpness in order to show the fine details of color and structure. In this photo some blurring has occured because of the slow shutter spead and the back and forth movement of the butterfly's wings. Photo taken in Durham, North Carolina with Coolpix 8700 camera. ISO 50, F4.1, 1/70 sec.

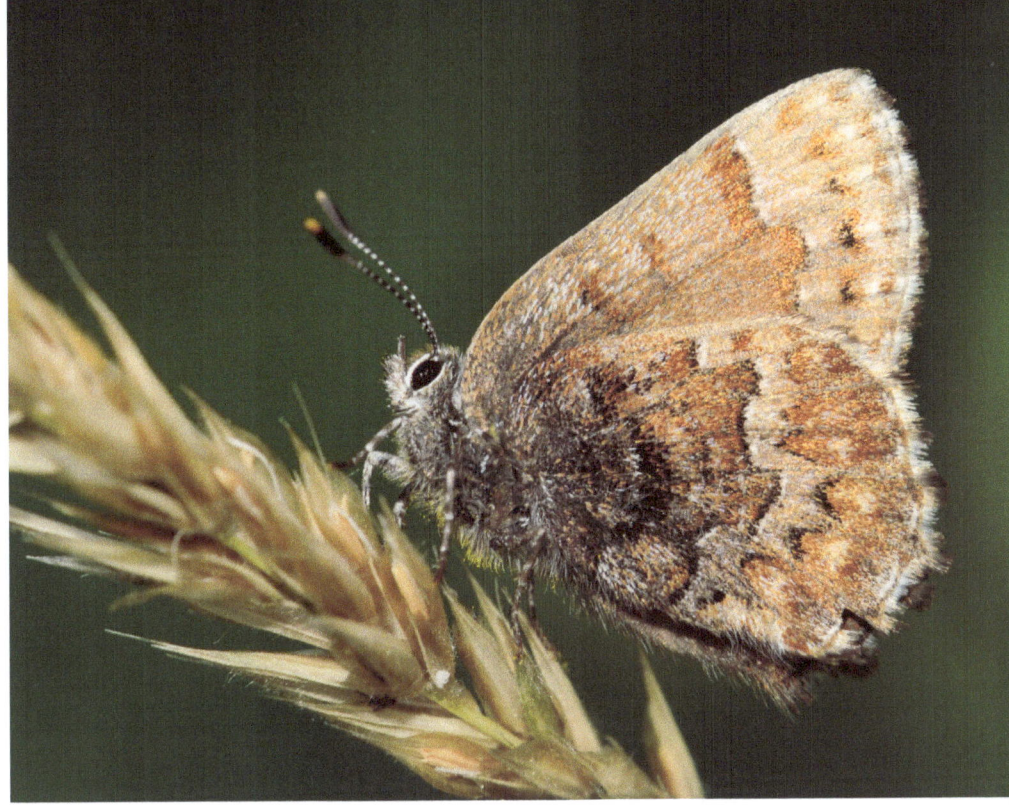

Small butterflies, such as this Eastern Pine Elfin (*Callophrys niphon*), are often difficult to approach closely. A DSLR camera with a telephoto lens improves the chances of photographing these butterflies. The narrow depth of field lessens the likelihood of a distracting background. Photo taken in Camden, Maine. Nikon D300 with a 180 mm macro lens, ISO 400, F11, 1/250 sec.

cameras are replacing P&S cameras. At present, they are more expensive than P&S models with comparable features.

Digital SLR cameras

Overview

The term "single lens reflex" refers to the mirror system that allows the viewfinder to see through the lens, improving both the quality and accuracy of the image in the viewfinder. DSLRs also have larger sensors, which increases the sharpness of an image, all other aspects being equal. Because of the mirror system and larger sensors, DSLRs are generally bigger and heavier than P&S cameras, and they cost more for cameras with comparable features.

Of all the brands of DSLR cameras, Canon and Nikon stand out as the leaders in the field. They have more choices in cameras and lenses, but more importantly, their flash metering systems are arguably the best available. This feature is important for butterfly photography, because often one only has a brief moment to

obtain the right exposure, balancing ambient (background) light with fill flash. The camera needs to be able to "talk" to the flash and have the ability to be able to take exposure readings in the area on which the camera is focusing, as well as on the background.

Full frame versus compact DSLRs

The first choice one needs to make in deciding which DSLR to purchase is whether to invest in a full frame camera, which has approximately a 36x24 mm sensor, or a compact DSLR with a smaller sensor (23.5x15.6 mm in Nikon compact DSLRs). The larger sensor of full frame cameras has a greater light-gathering capacity and potentially greater clarity. The resulting image in the viewfinder is brighter, allowing easier manual focusing. Full frame cameras are better in low-light situations without a flash and can produce quality images at higher ISO values. Because the image has more pixels, it can be cropped to a greater degree without causing a noticeable loss of image quality. Full frame cameras are ideal for landscapes, wide-angle photography and sports/action photography.

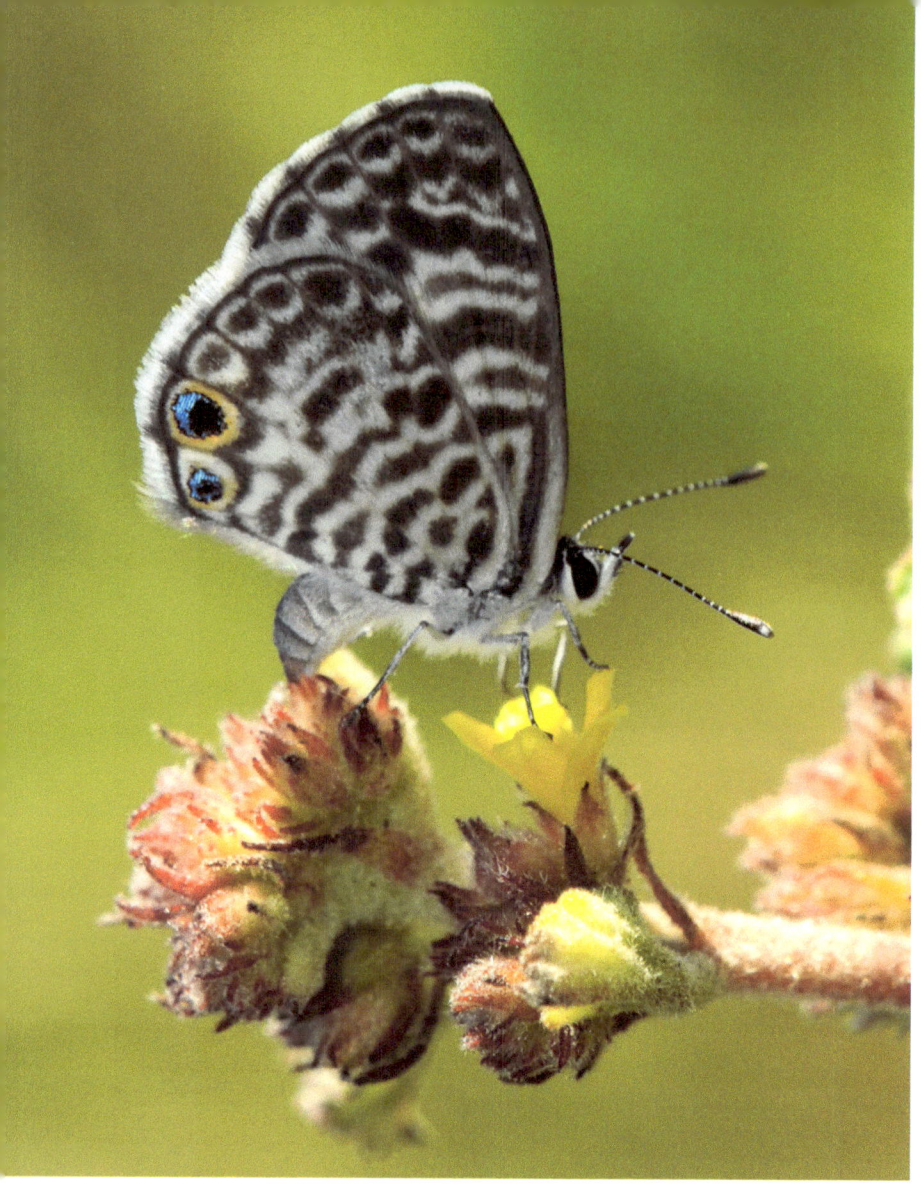

Blues are one of the most difficult butterflies to photograph. They are tiny, they spend most of their time flying erratically, and when they do land, it's only for a few seconds. This Cassius Blue ((*Leptotes cassius*) may have taken a little extra time to oviposit (as shown by its curled abdomen). Fortunately, it also landed in a suitable orientation for a photograph. The rapid focus and narrow depth of field afforded by the DSLR camera and telephoto lens facilitated capturing this image. Photo taken at Eco Pond, Flamingo, Florida (Everglades National Park), Nikon D300 with 180 mm lens, ISO 640, F11, 1/640 sec.

However, the sensor is one of the most expensive parts of a camera, and full frame cameras cost more.

Compact DSLRs also take excellent photos, especially at the close ranges inherent to butterfly photography. Because the sensor is smaller, it uses only the central part of a full-frame lens and magnifies the image by about 50% (this is referred to as a "crop factor" of 1.5). What this means is that for any given lens, the apparent focal length will be 50% greater when used on a compact camera. For butterfly photography, this has the advantage that the photographer doesn't need to be as close to the butterfly. Because lenses designed for compact DSLRs project onto a smaller sensor, they can be smaller, lighter and less expensive. Compact cameras

can use full frame lenses and vice versa. In the case of a compact camera and full frame lens, only the central part of a full frame lens is used. In the case of a full frame camera and compact lens, only the central part of the larger sensor can be used (there is no magnification; just fewer pixels).

My recommendation: if budget is not an issue, buy a full frame system for its greater flexibility. For the rest of us, compact DSLRs will provide excellent butterfly photographs at a lower cost. Butterfly photographs are usually taken during the daytime with ample light using autofocus, and the increased magnification of the 1.5 crop factor inherent to compact cameras is a plus.

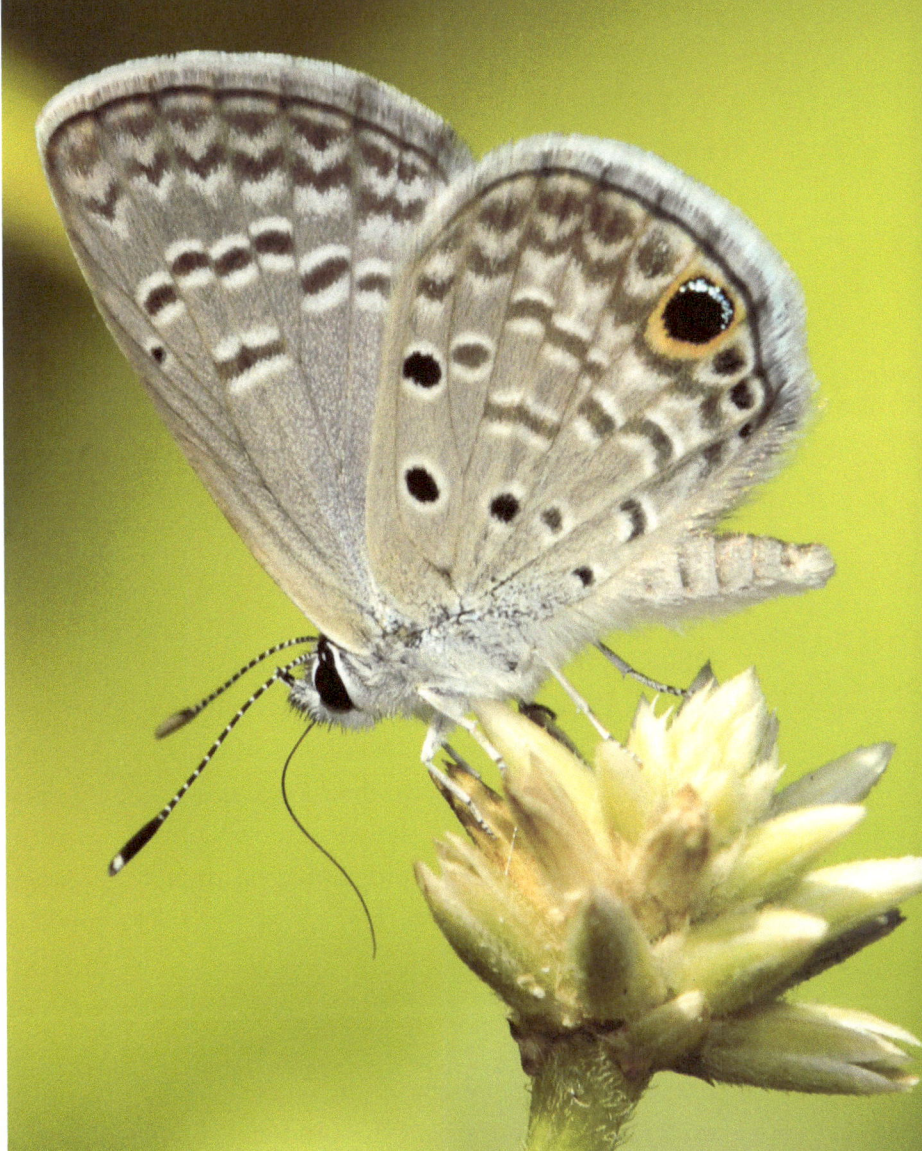

In addition to being hard to photograph, many blues look similar. This Ceraunus Blue (*Hemiargus ceraunus*) is difficult to distinguish from the Cassius Blue (opposite page) in flight, and even at rest one needs to look carefully at the pattern of markings to tell the two apart. Photographs are the best way to be sure. Photo taken in Everglades National Park, Flamingo, Florida, Nikon D300 camera, ISO 640, F11, 1/800 sec.

Focusing

One advantage of DSLR systems is the rapidity of the autofocus mechanism. Although one can focus manually, it is difficult enough to hold the camera still when trying to focus on a moving insect. In my opinion, for butterfly photography it is worth paying more money for a camera with a good autofocusing system, and is one of the reasons I prefer DSLRs to P&S cameras. On my camera (Nikon D300), I choose continuous autofocus, so if the butterfly or I move, the camera will adjust, and spot focusing which allows me to choose the point on which the camera focuses. Alternatively, I may choose "dynamic-area autofocus", for which I have chosen 3D tracking in the menu. This allows me to focus on the butterfly and then re-compose the image with the camera keeping the butterfly in focus, regardless of where I place it in the photo. The bottom line here is to take the time to learn the details of whatever camera you are using. Often the Users' Manuals are not well-written, but excellent explanations are available on the Web.

Image stabilization

Image stabilization (IS; vibration reduction) is another nice-to-have feature. Using a tripod is usually impractical with butterfly photography, increasing the ISO is limited by noise, and increasing the shutter speed is limited by available light. IS generally allows photographs to be taken at shutter speeds ½ to ¼ of that needed for a non-stabilized system, or, put another way, results in fewer blurred images at any given shutter speed. Two types of IS exist: optical IS in the lens (Canon and Nikon) and sensor-based IS in the camera (Sony, Pentax, Olympus). There is a debate over which is better. Camera-based stabilization can be used with multiple lenses and is therefore less expensive in the long run. However, it is unlikely that Canon or Nikon will ever change to a camera-based system, now that they have produced multiple lenses with IS.

In summary, the most important aspects of DSLR cameras are the size and quality of the sensors, the accuracy of the light metering system, and the rapidity and accuracy of autofocus. DSLRs are more expensive than P&S cameras, but if one's budget will allow it, they will provide a more satisfying photographic experience with fewer "missed" shots.

Lenses

The lens is as important as the camera (some would say more important) for producing high-quality images. The colors on a butterfly usually have sharp borders, and any lack of crispness will be readily perceived in a photograph. The minute structures on a butterfly, such as the details of its eye or the hairs on its thorax, can only be reproduced adequately by a lens with a high degree of sharpness.

The optical characteristics of a lens depend on a series of glass or plastic elements used to focus the beam of light onto the sensor. These elements are coated to minimize chromatic aberration (different wavelengths of light focusing at different points, creating colored fringes along lines of contrast) and to maximize contrast (the ability to distinguish between similar hues). Chromatic aberration is magnified in macro photography and in the bright, contrasting colors often seen in a butterfly's wings. Together,

the ability to minimize chromatic aberration and maximize contrast are key components making up the sharpness of a lens, which is the single most important feature of a lens for butterfly photography.

The overall construction of a lens is a major component of the cost of the lens. Inexpensive lenses are made of plastic bodies and are less rugged. High quality lenses are made of aluminum or other metals. It is not surprising that the lenses with the best (and most expensive) optics are enclosed in high quality housings.

All lenses are compromises between different ideals. There is no perfect lens for butterfly photography (or for any other type of photography). In general, a telephoto macro lens is best. Telephoto lenses allow the photographer to photograph from a distance and minimize the likelihood that the butterfly will be spooked. However, longer focal length lens must have a greater diameter to compensate for the reduced light reaching the sensor. It will be more difficult to hold the camera still, and any camera motion will be magnified. Focal lengths between 100 and 200 millimeters are best, and even these focal lengths require excellence in photographic technique (holding the camera still). The "macro" aspect of the lens refers to the ability of the lens to focus close enough to provide a 1:1 (life size) image of the subject on the sensor. Zoom lenses (ones that can vary the effective focal length) are not ideal. They are unnecessary for butterfly photography and require more lens elements, resulting in greater weight, less light transmission and images that are not as sharp.

The "speed" of a lens refers to its ability to transmit light, with faster lenses able to transmit more light at their maximum aperture. In general, the higher the quality of the elements within the lens, the faster will be the lens. Of course, the overall lens diameter is also important, with smaller diameter lenses transmitting less light. The speed of a lens is rated according to the "F" number achieved when the lens is wide open with a smaller F number signifying a faster lens. For butterfly photography an F number of 3.5 or less is best. One needs to balance speed with the weight and size of a lens needed to achieve the faster speeds.

An autofocus lens is essential for butterfly photography. It is too difficult to hold the camera still enough for close-up butterfly photography and to manually focus at the same time. Although a fast focusing lens is a plus, accuracy is more important than speed. The ideal lens is able to shift rapidly between manual and auto-

focus. In that manner, one can focus manually to get close, and then switch to autofocus for fine tuning. Many macro lenses have a switch that limits the focus range, allowing the camera to focus more rapidly within the designated range.

As mentioned earlier, a camera/lens system with vibration reduction is a plus, but is not essential. If the vibration reduction is part of the lens, the lens will be larger and more expensive.

The "bokeh" of a lens is worth paying attention to. This refers to the ability of the lens to produce a smooth out-of-focus background, rather than a clutter of bright circles. There are no standards for measuring or quantifying bokeh. I mention it here, because you will often see it

An extreme case of poor bokeh. This photo of a Horace's Duskinging (*Erynnis horatius*) was taken with a Nikon Coolpix 990, an early point-and-shoot camera. Rather than smoothing the background, the camera exaggerated the highlights, creating a mass of out-of-focus circles. ISO 100, F5.6, 1/150 sec.

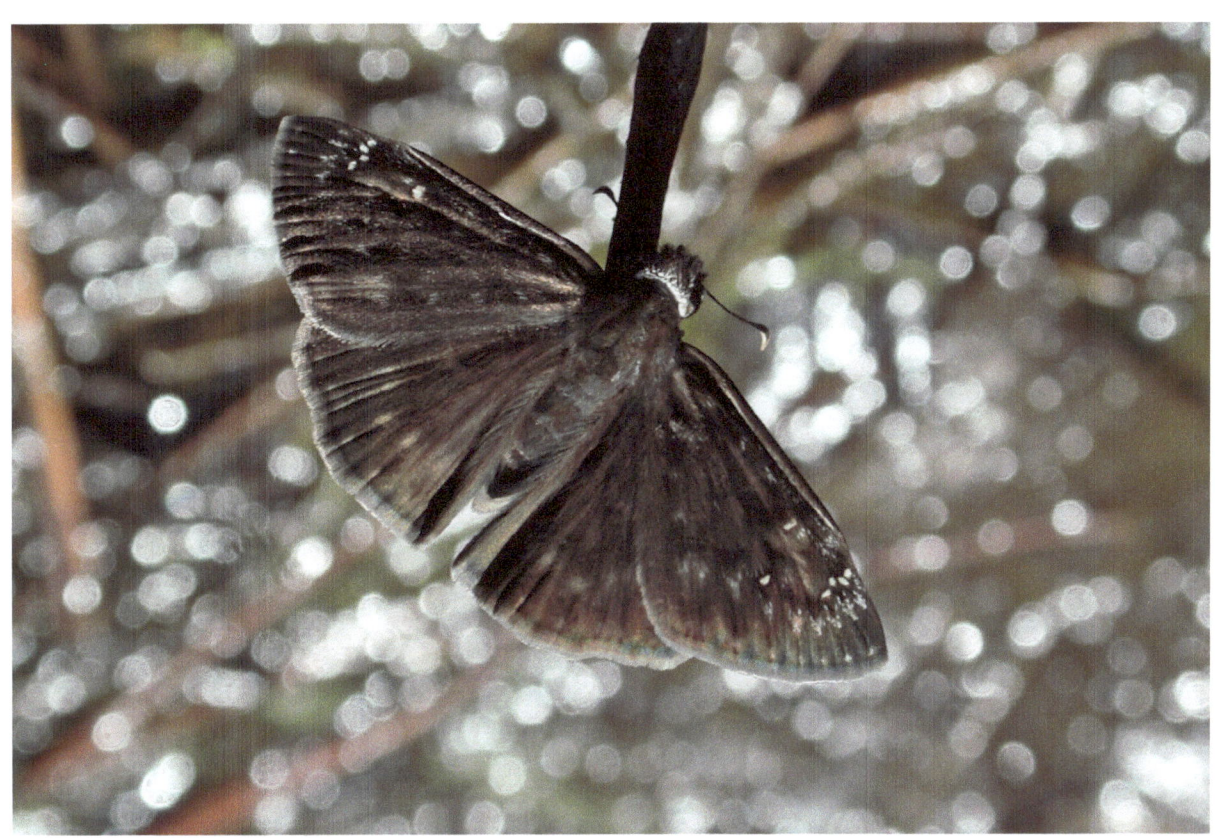

referred to in reviews of lenses.

There are several options for aspiring butterfly photographers who don't have, or cannot afford, a telephoto macro lens. Although I use a 180 mm macro lens, one can substitute a 100-120 mm macro lens on a compact DSLR, which will provide an effective focal length of about 150-180 mm due to the approximately 1.5x crop factor. Using the shorter lens on a full frame DSLR will not provide sufficient telephoto power for most butterfly photography.

Another option for achieving macro capability with a standard telephoto lens is to screw on a close-up filter to the front of the lens. Such filters act like magnifying glasses, with the strength of magnification being measured in diopters (analogous to reading glasses). The most common sizes are +2 to +4 diopters. The greater the number of diopters, the closer one can focus, but also the more limited will be the maximum focus distance. The advantage of close-up filters is that they can easily be taken on or off the lens. Because they place additional glass in front of the camera, it is important to get the best quality filter(s) possible. Inexpensive close-up filters can degrade image quality significantly. These filters are not a good solution for short telephoto lenses (under 100 mm), because they require that the camera be placed too close to the butterfly.

One option that I do not recommend for butterfly photography is to place an extension tube between the camera and lens. The greater the length of the extension tube, the closer the camera can focus, and the greater the degree of magnification. However, extension tubes do not provide much magnification for longer telephoto lenses and prevent the lens from focusing on distant objects. Extension tubes require removal of the lens from the camera, which, in

the field, increases the risk of getting dust on the sensor. For butterfly photography, it would be necessary to purchase an extension tube that maintains the electronic connection between the lens and the camera; otherwise, the camera will be unable to communicate with the lens and autofocus will be impossible. Extension tubes are mainly used in macro-photography in conjunction with a tripod. In such situations, autofocus is unnecessary and a simple (non-electronic) extension tube is sufficient.

Finally, one can place a 1.4 - 2.0 teleconverter between the camera and the lens to increase the effective focal length of the lens. For example, a 100 mm lens with a 1.7x teleconverter will have an effective focal length of 170 mm. Because more glass is placed in front of the sensor, it is important to get the best quality teleconverter possible. Teleconverters will not decrease the minimum focus distance of the lens. They will reduce the speed of autofocus, and because they reduce the amount of light reaching the camera, the autofocus may not work well, especially at high F stops.

In summary, the quality of the sensor and lens are the two most important features of a camera system for butterfly photography. It is worth investing in a telephoto macro lens if ones budget will allow it.

Flashes

Butterfly photography is usually enhanced by the use of a flash. Although some photographers will disagree with this statement, it forms a foundation of how I approach butterfly photography. Assuming there is adequate ambient light, the flash serves to soften the shadows, diminish color shifts created by light reflecting off flowers or leaves, and enhance the color of the butterfly. When used in this manner it is called "fill flash". If there is insufficient ambient light, the flash becomes primary. In this case the butterfly is well lit, but the background will be dark. Although this situation can result in a dramatic photograph, the lighting may be harsher.

For P&S cameras, I recommend using the smallest flash available for the camera. Even so, many camera/flash combinations can't reduce the flash power sufficiently to avoid burning out close-up subjects. In this case, you'll need to use the flash in manual mode, often at 1/16 power or less. This is not as difficult as it might seem, and you'll quickly learn to adjust the flash depending on how far you will be from the butterfly and to use more flash for darker butterflies. You'll also need to use a flash diffuser, to soften the light coming from the flash. The diffuser is usually included as part of the flash. A high quality diffuser is unnecessary, as the amount of light coming from the flash is minimal. Once

A camera, lens and flash should have the ability to balance background exposure with proper illumination of the subject. In this photograph of a Juniper Hairstreak (*Callophrys gryneus*) backlit by the sun, the camera measured the background lighting, and the flash was used as a fill flash. Because of the strongly lit background, I bracketed the camera exposure, and the +0.3 stop exposure compensation turned out best. I generally set the flash to an exposure compensation of -0.3 to -0.7 stops to minimize the chance of creating over-exposed areas on the butterfly. Photo taken on Mount Lemmon, Arizona with a Nikon D300 camera and a Nikon SB-900 flash, ISO 400, F11, 1/320 sec.

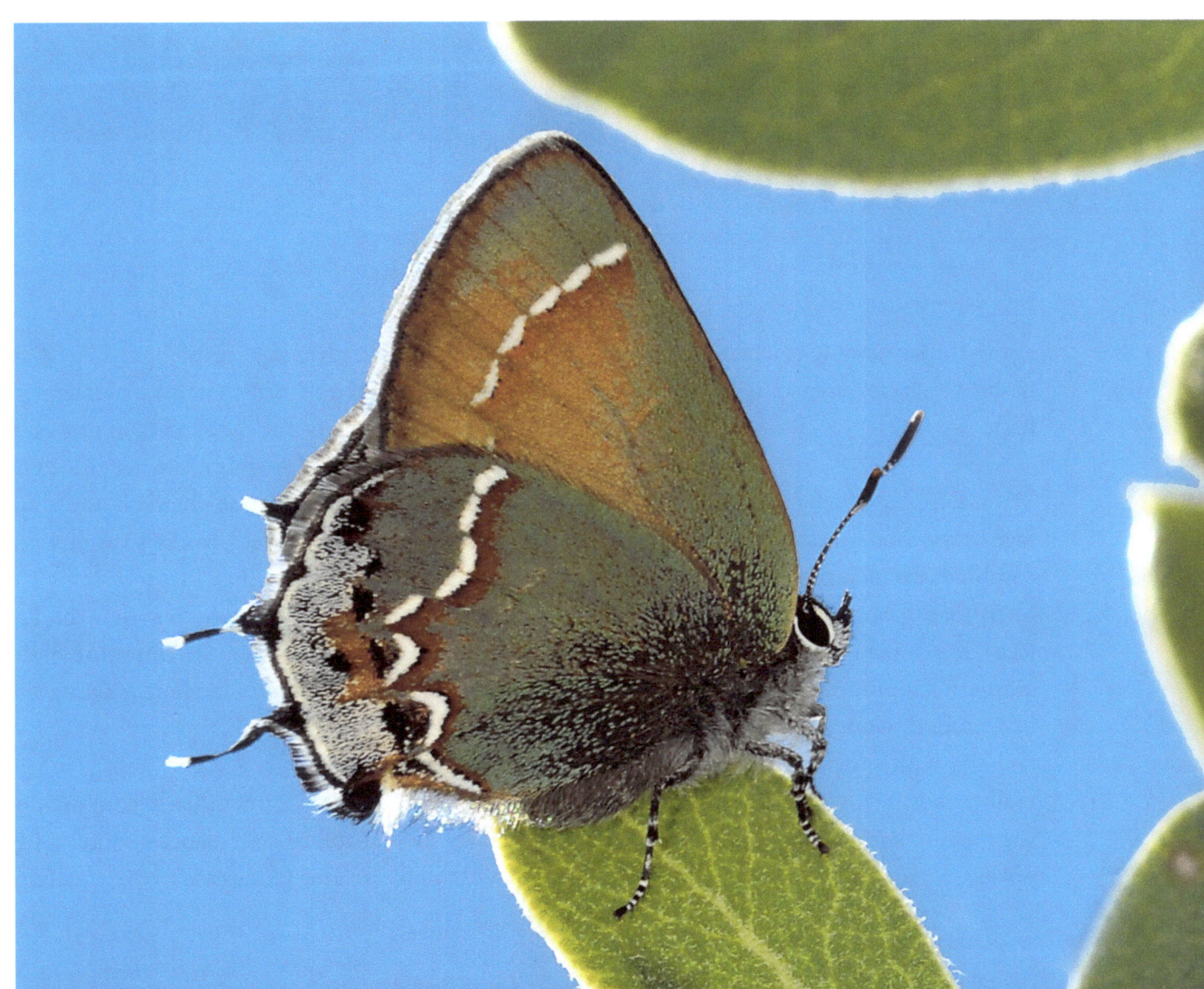

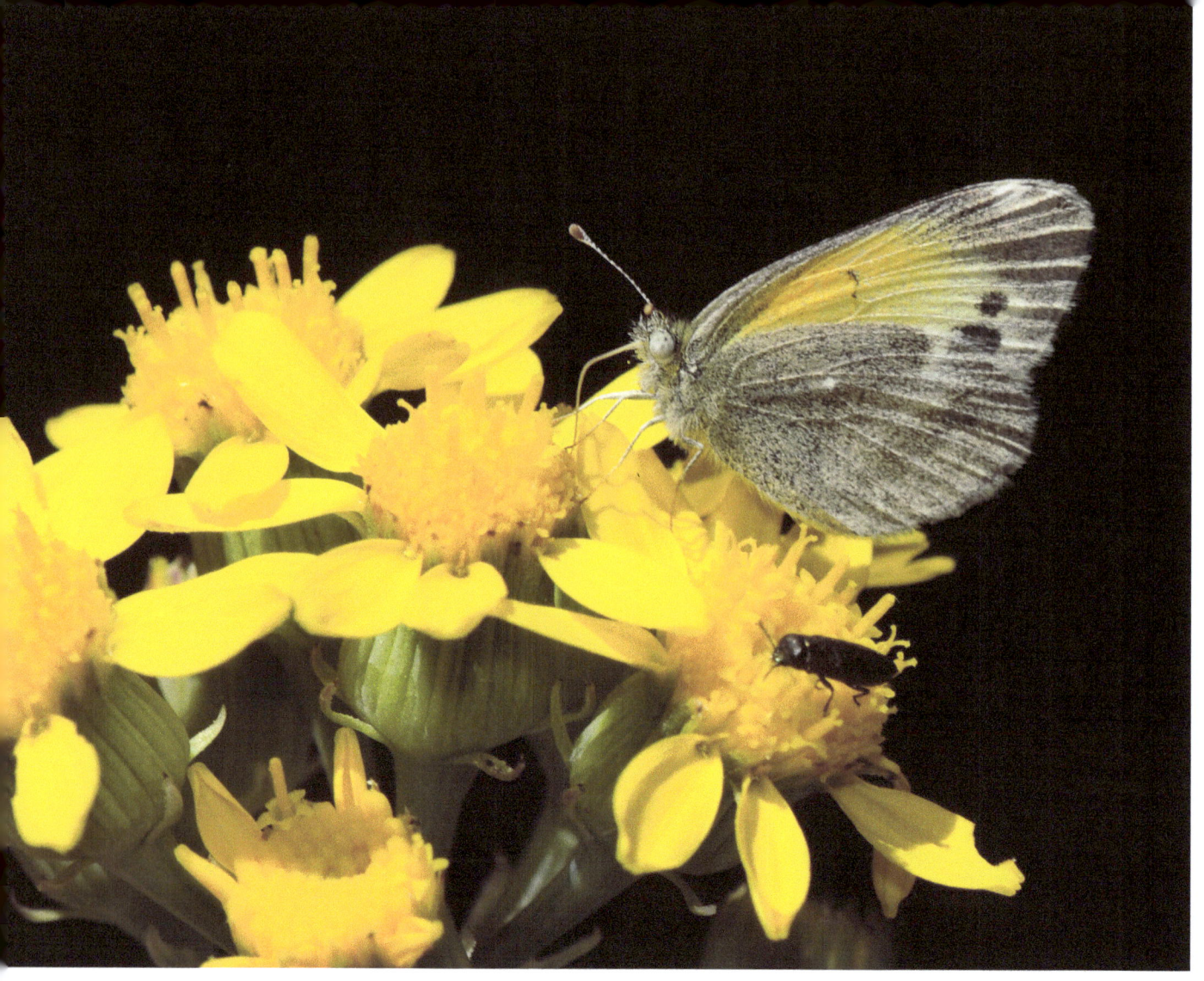

In this photograph of a Dainty Sulphur (*Nathalis iole*) taken in the shade, the background was underexposed, causing the flash to become the primary light source. Under these conditions, it is best to use a flash diffuser to soften the light hitting the subject. Photo taken with a Nikon D300 camera and SB-900 flash, ISO 400, F11, 1/800 sec with a camera exposure compensation of -0.3 stops.

again, the key is to start with a small, low power flash, which, in essence, is being used as a fill flash.

With DSLRs, photographers can take advantage of the modern camera/flash systems, which combine two metering systems, one for the ambient (background) light, and one for the subject. The camera measures the ambient light to create the appropriate exposure settings for the background, sends this information to the flash, and the flash provides sufficient light to optimally expose the subject. Because the butterfly is generally within a few feet of the camera, a powerful flash is unnecessary, although there

is also no disadvantage to using a large flash. As long as there is sufficient ambient light, all one needs to do is put the camera in one of the automatic modes (program, shutter-priority or aperture-priority), turn on the flash and shoot. I have found this system works so well with a telephoto macro lens that in most cases I no longer need a flash diffuser to soften the light from the flash. However, the closer the flash is to the subject, the more likely it is that a flash diffuser will be beneficial.

Of course, not all camera/flash combinations have the capability to balance ambient light with fill flash. This is one case where you'll need to do some experimentation to see what works best with your camera, lens and flash combination.

A different situation arises when there is insufficient ambient light to provide an acceptable combination of F-stop and shutter speed. Then, the flash becomes the primary light source. This situation can be expected for butterflies in woodland locations and commonly occurs in tropical jungles. In these instances, I typically put the camera in manual mode, set the shutter speed to the flash sync speed (1/250 sec) and set the aperture to around F10. The flash then decides how much light is needed, and any exposure compensation is done using the controls on the flash.

The above discussion pertains to a flash mounted on the camera's hot shoe. I have not tried ring flashes attached to the end of the lens or flashes mounted on a bracket. Because the camera is usually at least a couple of feet from the butterfly, I do not envision that a ring flash would provide a significant advantage.

One concept that is frequently misunderstood is the flash sync speed. At shutter speeds up to the flash's sync speed, the first shutter curtain opens, the flash fires, and the second shutter curtain closes. At speeds higher than the flash's sync speed, the second curtain begins to close before the first curtain is entirely open. Because the flash exposure lasts only about 1/1000 second, at high shutter speeds only part of the image is exposed. In camera/flash systems that have a high speed sync (HSS) mode, this problem is circumvented by extending the flash duration using a rapid series of pulses (e.g., 50,000 pulses/second). In this manner, the image is evenly exposed at any shutter speed, albeit at a greatly reduced effective flash output. As an example, if the flash duration is extended to 1/250 second in HSS and one is shooting at 1/2000 second, the effective flash power is reduced at least 8 fold (250/2000). This is a common situation in butterfly photography, in which there is ample light for fast shutter speeds. Because the butterfly is close to the camera, the reduction in effective flash output with HSS usually does not prevent an adequate exposure. The only real disadvantage to using HSS is that much of the flash output is wasted, and the flash batteries will not last as long. However, if one does not use HSS, the camera will reduce the shutter speed to the flash sync value (generally 1/200 – 1/250 second), and the image may be overexposed. In this situation one must decrease the lens aperture (increase F stop) to compensate for the slower shutter speed.

For those who want more detail on using flashes, a simple explanation of Canon's flashes can be found at (http://www.learn.usa.canon.com/resources/articles/2011/fill_flash_use_EOS_article.shtml). For Nikon's Creative Lighting System, an in depth review can be found on Russell MacDonald's blog (http://nikonclspracticalguide.blogspot.com/2008/01/).

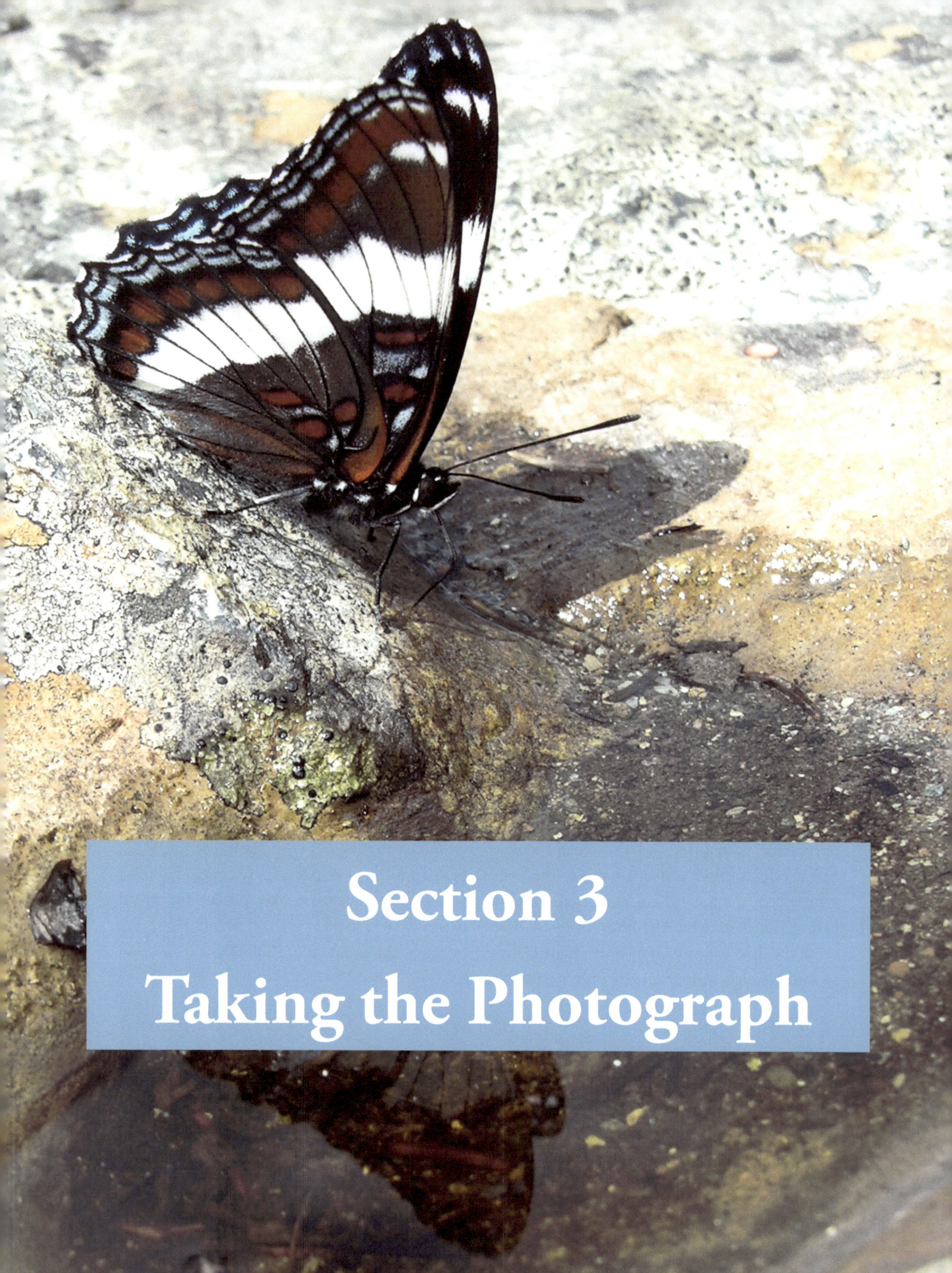

Section 3
Taking the Photograph

Combining Camera, Lens and Flash

Now that we've discussed the various components of a photographic system for butterfly photography, how are they used together? The photographer is fortunate, in that most butterflies prefer bright sunlight. This means that there is generally ample light to photograph the butterfly at acceptable camera settings.

Before going into the field, be sure to check all the settings on the camera to ensure they are optimal for the subject and conditions. What mode is the camera set on (program, aperture-priority, shutter-priority or manual)? Are the ISO, white balance, light meter, exposure compensation, focus and bracketing settings appropriate? Are the memory card and battery placed back in the camera? I have often been guilty of forgetting this checklist, and then wonder why the resulting images are not what I have expected.

At present, my equipment consists of a Nikon D300 camera, Tamron 180 mm macro lens and Nikon SB900 flash. I am wedded to the Nikon line because of the old manual Nikon lens that I still use on occasion. The D300 camera is a compact DSLR that utilizes Nikon's Creative Lighting System (the ability to balance ambient light with fill flash) and can do 3D focus tracking (keeping a moving object in focus), which is especially useful for photographing birds in flight. For butterfly photography, a camera of this quality is unnecessary, and other makes and models can produce excellent results. The choice of lens is important. I wanted a relatively long macro lens, because previously I had missed too many photographs trying to get too close to the butterfly. But using a 180 mm lens requires a steady hand, and this lens does not have vibration reduction. I wish I could say that I chose the Tamron lens after making an exhaustive trial of many lenses. In actuality, I took the recommendation of the excellent group of butterfly photographers in Singapore (http://butterflycircle.blogspot.com), with whom I had the good fortune to spend a day

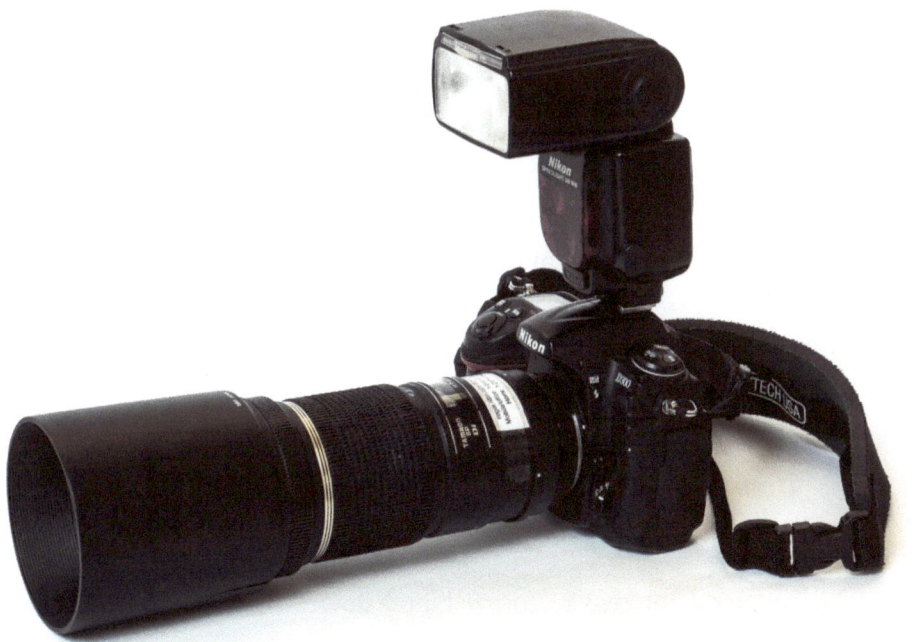

The author's current camera, lens and flash. See text for description.

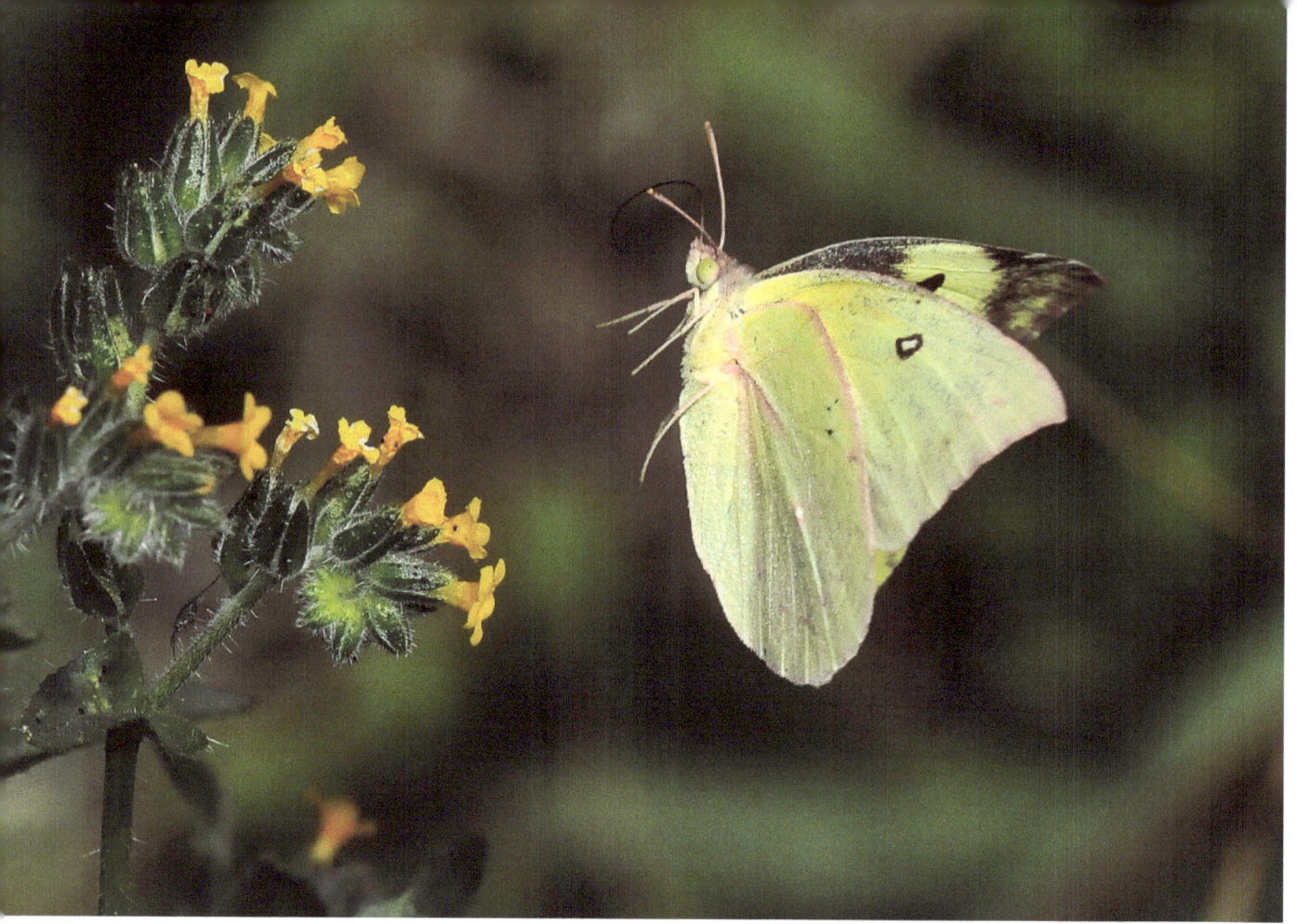

Southern Dogface (*Colias cesonia*) in flight. Photo taken using high-speed flash sychronization and a fast shutter speed to freeze the motion of the butterfly. Photo taken in Arivaipa Canyon, Arizona with Nikon D300 camera, ISO 800, F11, 1/4000 sec.

photographing butterflies. They all chose this lens based on its outstanding clarity and good bokeh (blurring of background out-of-focus areas). Besides not having vibration reduction, the lens' autofocus is mediocre. One needs to focus manually to get close, and then push the focus ring forward to engage the autofocus mechanism. After a little practice, this becomes a fast and efficient way of focusing quickly on a butterfly.

The front of the lens should be protected with a high quality, neutral density filter. After spending hundreds or thousands of dollars on a lens, one doesn't want to risk degrading the image with a low quality filter.

I always use a lens hood for two reasons. Not only does it help to avoid erroneous light readings from direct sunlight, it also helps to protect the front of the lens. Several times while concen-

trating on a subject, I have fallen, and the lens hood prevented the neutral density filter from being scratched.

The SB900 flash exceeds what is necessary for butterfly photography, but to get reliably good exposures, the camera and flash should be capable of balancing fill flash with ambient light. The SB900 flash has the ability to do high-speed flash synchronization, meaning that the flash will fire at any shutter speed (albeit at reduced effective power), which allows imaging of butterflies or moths in flight.

It is difficult to use a tripod for butterfly photography. Even if one is focused on a particular flower where butterflies are landing, they rarely land in an appropriate orientation to make use of a tripod. Under most conditions, I set the ISO on the camera at 400. This is usually sufficient sensitivity to allow for an adequately fast shutter speed. Under cloudy or shady conditions, I may increase the ISO to 800. With a full frame camera, one could go to a higher ISO. With my compact DSLR, higher settings risk having too much noise in the image, although in bright sunlight, noise is not usually a problem. I generally shoot in Aperture Priority mode, with the aperture set between F8 and F11. This is the "sweet spot" of the Tamron lens (and most other lenses), where the lens is the sharpest. However, if the butterfly is in a "congested" area, where it is difficult to shoot an uncluttered photo, I will reduce the F stop, in order to minimize depth of field and maximally blur the background.

I use "continuous autofocus" setting, so that when the shutter release is pressed half-way down, the camera will continuously adjust the focus should I move closer or further away from the butterfly. I use the "spot focus" setting, which allows me to select the focus point, and one of the matrix metering settings (full frame or center-weighted). The camera then adjusts

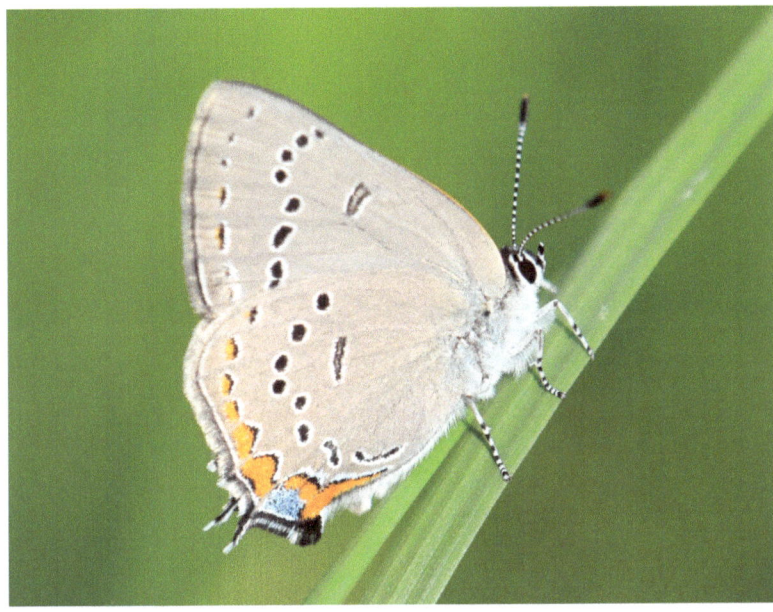

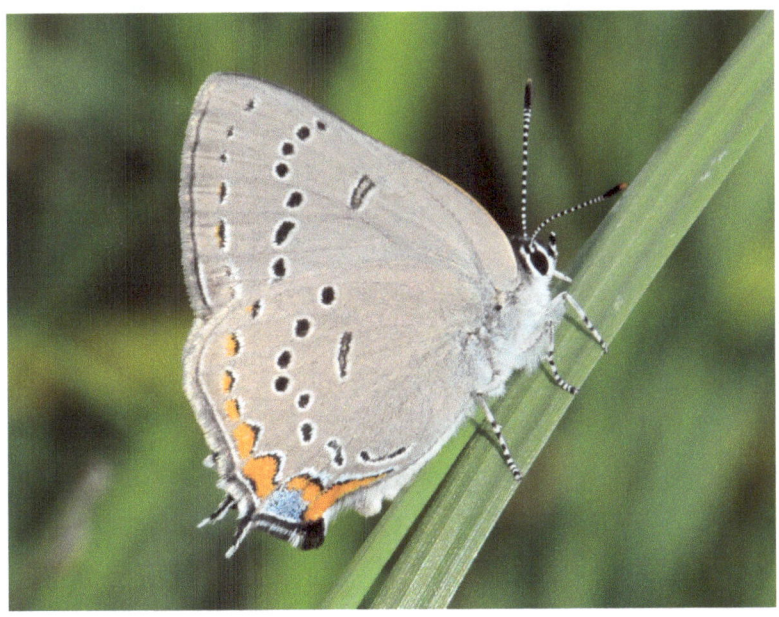

The effect of F stop on depth of field. The top photo of this Acadian Hairstreak (*Satyrium acadica*) was taken at F4 and the bottom photo at F22 (ISO 1000, shutter speed 1/8000 sec and 1/320 sec, respectively). Not only does the shallow depth of field remove the distracting background, but the excellent "bokeh" of the 180 mm Tamron lens results in a uniform yellowish-green background, free of bright highlights or dark shadows. Photos taken at the Camden Snow Bowl, Camden, Maine.

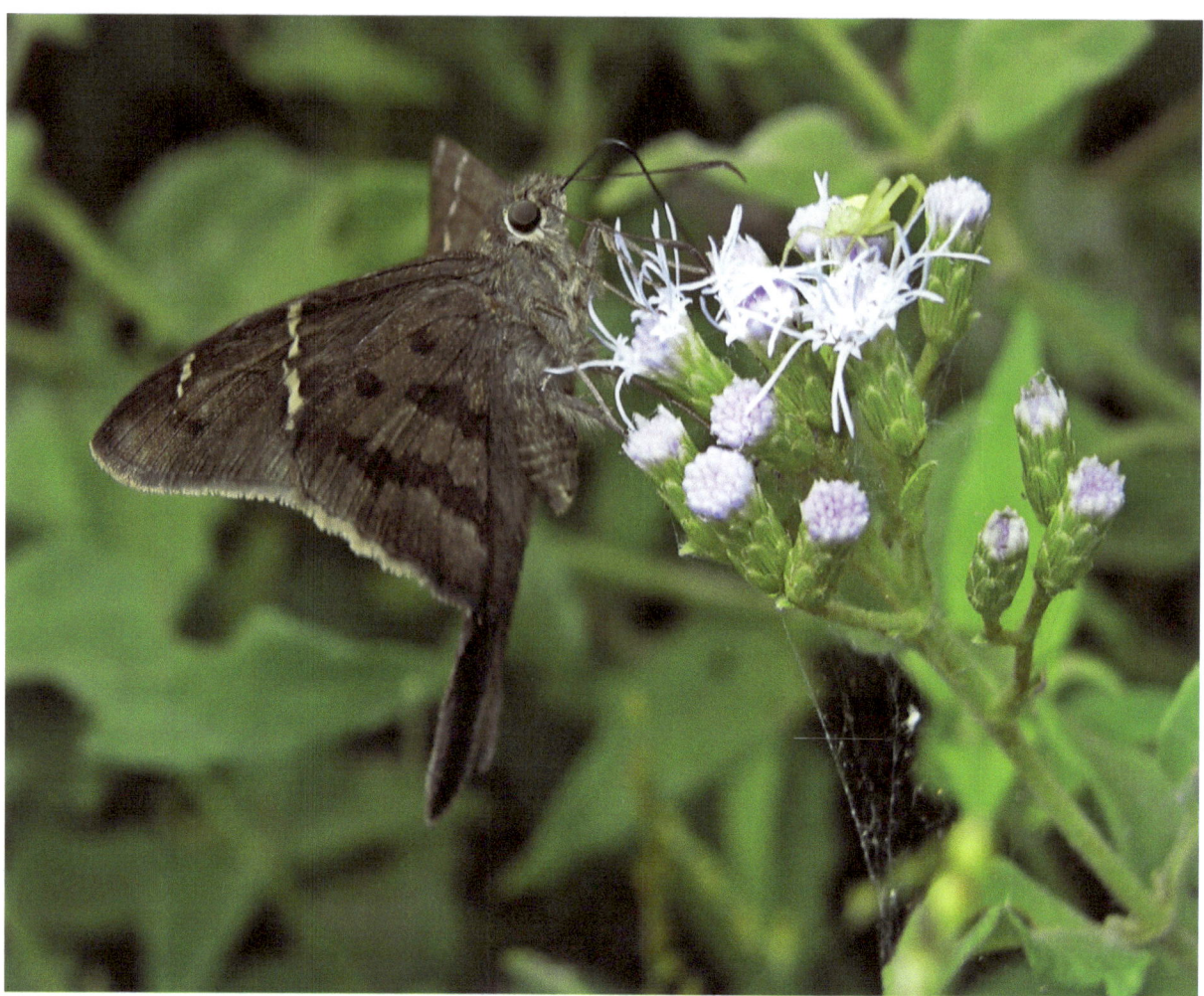

This photograph of a Brown Longtail (*Urbanus procne*) was taken with a Nikon Coolpix 8700 point-and-shoot camera at an aperture of F4. Note the distracting background caused by the large depth of field with the camera's lens, despite the low F-stop. Photo taken at the National Butterfly Center, Mission, Texas. ISO 50, F4, 1/110 sec.

the shutter speed to provide the optimal exposure for the ambient light. The flash is set at "TTL-BL" which is Nikon's fill flash setting.

After taking a photo, if the background is too light or dark, the exposure compensation on the camera can be adjusted. If the subject is too light or dark, the exposure compensation on the flash should be adjusted (assuming that you have a cooperative butterfly!). There are circumstances that require modifications of the above approach. These will be covered in the next section.

Should one shoot in RAW or JPEG? This is really a personal preference. If you want to do a lot of fine tuning of a photograph in programs such as Photoshop or Lightroom, it is best to shoot in RAW. For simple cropping, light adjustment and sharpening, JPEG usually suffices. Often I save images in both formats simultaneously, and then only save the RAW files of the couple of images that I think are real winners. I use the "fine" JPEG setting, the one with the least compression. Also, I shoot in the largest image size, 4288x2848 pixels on the D300 camera, knowing that I will be cropping the images later on.

Is there a need for bracketing exposures (taking 3 or more images at different exposures) to improve the chances of an optimal exposure?

Again, this is a personal preference, but with rapid feedback on the LCD screen/histogram and the benefits of adjusting the images on a computer, I rarely bother to bracket. It's really a matter of trying to minimize the amount of time spent discarding redundant images or trying to decide which image is actually the best.

What is the best way to judge exposure? If you can see the LCD screen clearly, the image on the LCD screen will give you a good sense of the overall exposure of the image. One does need to remember that in bright light, the LCD image will look darker than in subdued light or shadow. The histogram is necessary to show if a small part of the image is overexposed. Most cameras today have a playback option where one can see both the image and associated histogram. An example of an image and its associated histogram is shown below.

If one saw this butterfly photograph on an LCD screen, one might suspect that some areas of the flowers in the foreground were overexposed. The histogram is the proof. The white area of the histogram shows the relative number of pixels (vertical axis) at any given light value, with darkest values on the left and lightest values on the right. The peak on the left side of the histogram (blue arrow) represents the dark butterfly, and the large peaks on the right represent the background and light-colored flowers. Importantly, there are white bars at both the left and right edges of the histogram (orange arrows). The bar on the left represents black areas devoid of any light. The bar on the right represents totally white areas where the image has been overexposed, in this case the highlights of the flowers. Small pure black areas usually are not distracting, such as the black markings on the butterfly. Pure white areas look bad, and there

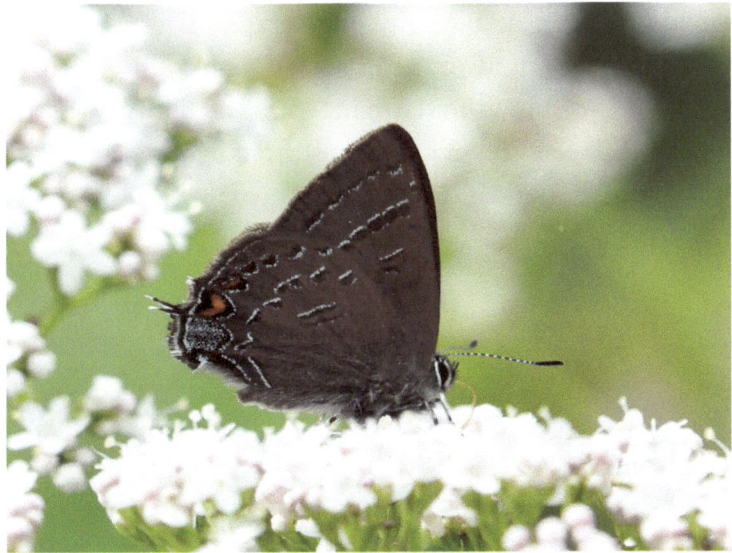

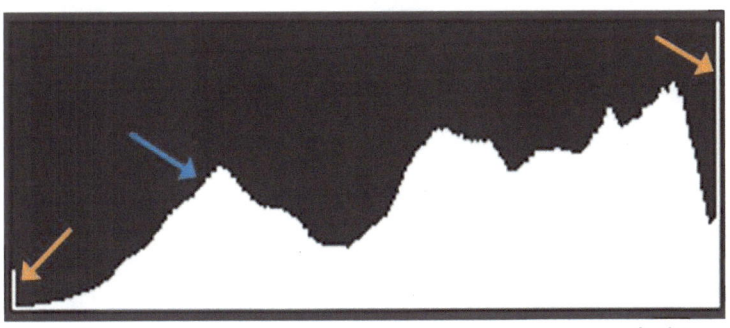

dark   light

Banded Hairstreak (*Satyrium calanus*) and associated histogram. See text for explanation. Photo taken in Camden, Maine. Nikon D300 camera, 180 mm macro lens, ISO 1000, F 11, 1/400 sec, +1 step exposure compensation.

is no way to recover color from these overexposed areas. The histogram indicates that the image is overexposed. Why did this happen? In order to adequately expose the butterfly, I had set the exposure compensation on the camera to +1 stop. Sometimes it is impossible to properly exposure both very light and very dark areas of the same image, especially when they are both part of the foreground. In those cases it is usually better to ensure that the highlights are not overexposed. The dark areas can be lightened later using an imaging processing program on a computer.

White balance is the adjustment that allows the camera to see a white object as white. During the middle of the day, the sun provides a neutral white balance. Shade tends to make white look bluish, whereas incandescent lights create a yellowish cast. The human brain adjusts to interpret white as white, regardless of whether the source of light is shade, bright sun or indoor incandescent lights.

The white balance of light is measured on a Kelvin temperature scale, with 5000 degrees being neutral light. Higher values indicate progressively more "cool" (bluish) light, and lower values indicate a light that has a "warm" color cast (yellow/orange/red). Using the camera's "automatic" white balance setting, the camera attempts to adjust to any perceived white imbalance. For example, in a cloudy or shady situation (6500-10,000 Kelvin), the camera will shift the white balance to a warmer color setting. In situations where the automatic white balance setting doesn't produce the desired effect, the photographer can specify the white balance in the camera (e.g., using the "cloudy" setting for overcast days or by choosing a specific Kelvin temperature). Alternatively, the white balance can be adjusted on a computer using programs such as Photoshop or Lightroom.

With butterfly photography, the automatic white balance setting produces acceptable results virtually all of the time. This is probably because butterfly photography is usually done in bright sun, and the fill flash's white balance is similar to daylight. Also the fill flash lessens the effect of a color cast from light reflecting off flowers or leaves.

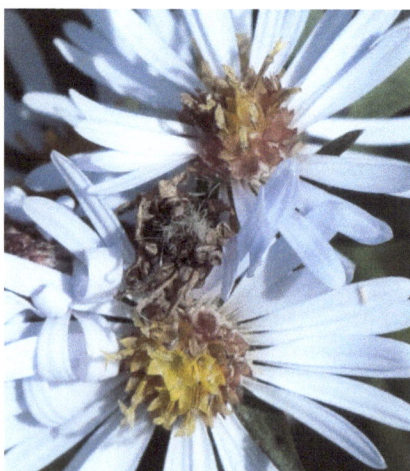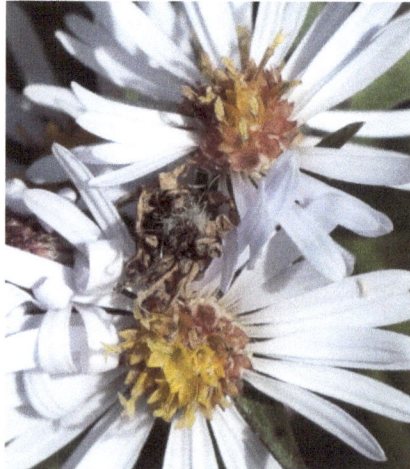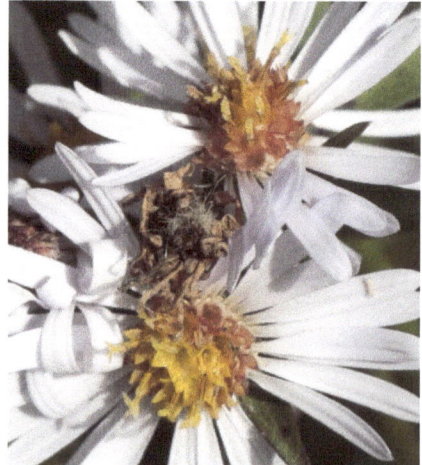

Image of pale bluish-purple New York Asters photographed in full sun without a flash at midday in raw format, and the white balance adjusted in Adobe Camera Raw to Kelvin 4000 (left), 5000 (center) and 6000 (right). There is a shift from a bluish to reddish cast to adjust for the white balance bias that would have occurred if the ambient light were at each of these values. Nikon D300, ISO 400, F10, 1/1250 sec.

What to Bring into the Field

Generally, the sunnier and warmer the weather, the more the butterflies like it. Under such circumstances, a light-weight, long-sleeved shirt and long pants are important as protection from the sun and noxious plants and insects. But-terflies have excellent color vision, including in the ultraviolet range, and wearing earth tones is probably less likely to distract a butterfly. Fortunately, sunscreen and insect repellant don't seem to repel the butterflies, at least at the distance between them and the camera. A baseball cap is useful to shade the sun, although it will need

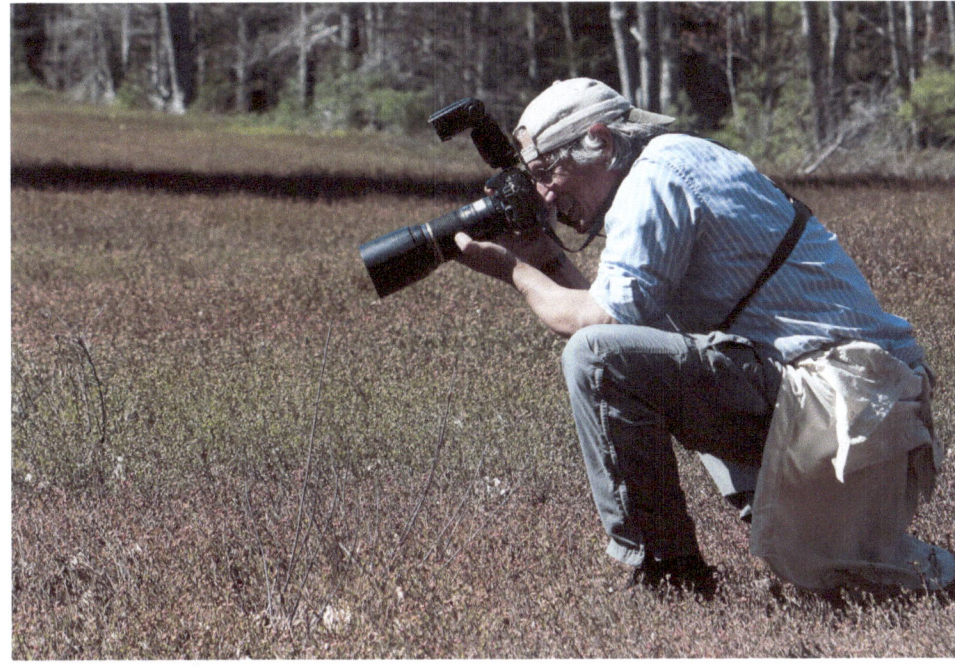

The author attempting to photograph Brown Elfins (*Callophrys augustinus*) in a blueberry field in Maine ... (Photo courtesy of Jeannie Hutchins)

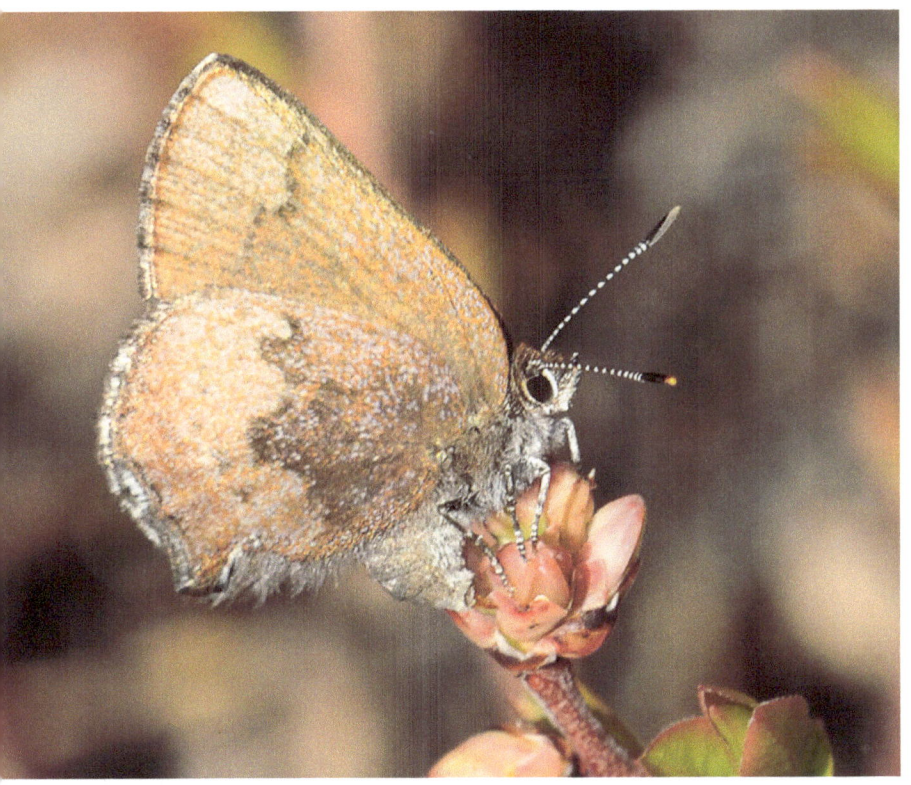

... and the result (after cropping). The Elfin is about to oviposit on the bud of the blueberry flower, its host plant. The egg has not yet appeared, but the curled abdomen is visible with an opening at the end. Nikon D300 camera, 180 mm macro lens: ISO 640, F 10, 1/640 sec.

A knowledge of the natural history of a butterfly increases the odds of obtaining a good photograph. In this case, this West Virginia White (*Pieris virginiensis*) was nectaring on its host plant, Cut-leaved Toothwort (*Cardamine concatenata*). West Virginia Whites only fly in the spring, and like most Whites, they seldom land for very long. However, the combination of a morning chill in early April and the presence of its host plant caused this White to pause long enough for a close-up photograph. Photo taken in Graham County, North Carolina. Nikon Coolpix 8700 camera, ISO 50, F4.4, 1/250 sec.

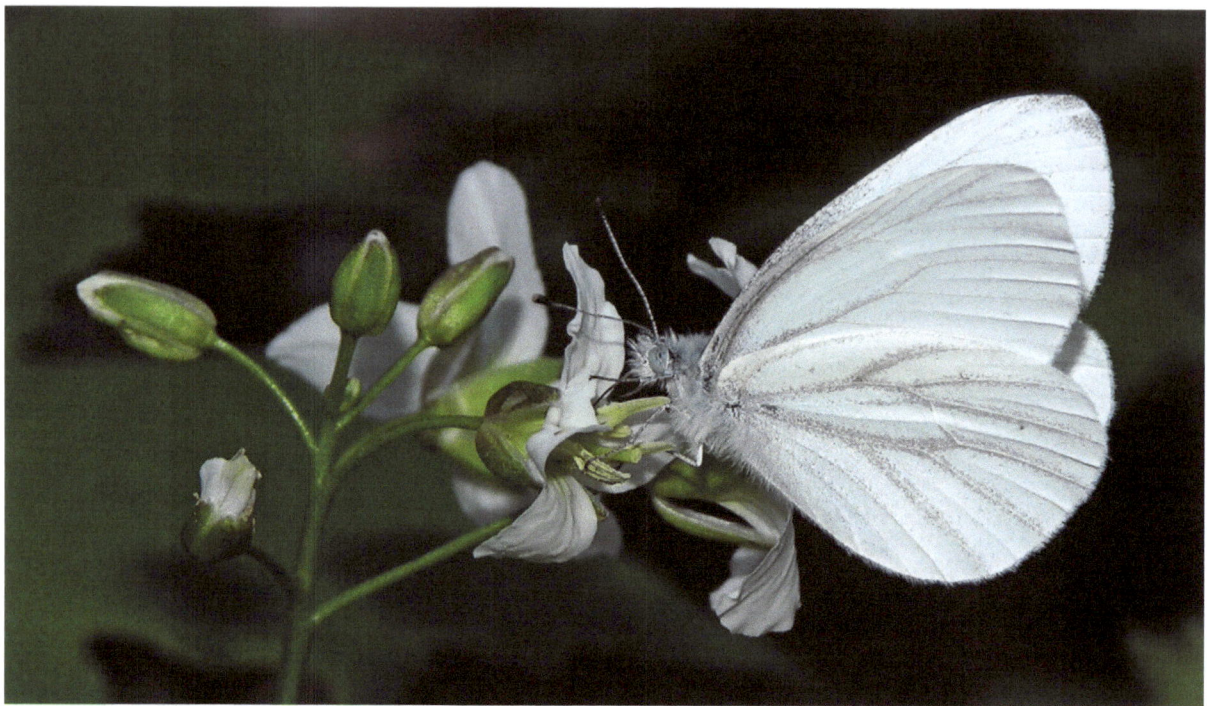

to be put on backwards when actually taking photos with a DSLR camera. Otherwise, the visor will knock into the flash. Close-focusing binoculars are helpful in identifying butterflies. I wear mine strapped to a chest harness, so as not to interfere with my camera. A waterproof bag is important to avoid ruining camera equipment in an unanticipated downpour. If I am wearing a day pack, I usually pack a butterfly field guide. There are also butterfly apps for smartphones, but they are not as user-friendly when trying to compare two similar butterflies. Finally, I often carry some water to avoid dehydration and overheating.

Picture-taking Tips

The first instinct of a novice photographer (and some not-so-novices) is to rapidly approach a new butterfly to get the first photo. Often, this results in a poor photo or a butterfly that is quickly spooked. A better approach is to watch the butterfly and learn its habits. Does it fly quickly from one flower to another? How does it hold its wings? Does it quickly rotate on a flower or stay in one position? Is it easily distracted by other insects or wind? To optimize the chance of a good photograph, there is no substitute for an intimate knowledge of the butterfly's habits. Such information will let you know how close you can get before creating a flight reaction. In the end, slow deliberate movements will likely yield the best photographic opportunities. If you are uncertain how close a butterfly can be approached, it is best to start taking pictures at a distance and then gradually move closer.

Two things that are almost certain to scare off a butterfly are shadows and exhaled air. Both simulate a predator. Therefore, it is important to avoid letting a shadow from your body or camera fall on the butterfly. And if a butterfly can sense your breath, you are too close. When approaching a butterfly, one must step carefully to avoid stepping on a stick or branch that then causes movement of the plant where the butterfly is resting. This is easier said than done, because one's vision is usually glued to the butterfly. Fortunately, butterflies cannot hear, although they feel vibrations well. Talking in a moderate voice will not frighten a butterfly. Sometimes it is possible to stand still and let the butterflies come to you. In such cases, it is helpful to be sitting or kneeling to start with, in order not to scare the butterfly when trying to squat. Even with all of these precautions, many butterflies are exquisitely attuned to predators and can be frustratingly sensitive to a photographer's presence.

Butterfly photography is more demanding than many other types of photography, because of the intricacy of the color patterns on a butterfly's wings and the minute details of its body parts. It is important to hold the camera as still as possible while pressing the shutter release. Any blurring will be noticeable to some degree. Using vibration reduction and a fast shutter speed is helpful, but these will not replace good photographic technique. Sometimes the camera can be braced against an object. Otherwise, gripping the (DSLR) camera firmly with both hands and holding it close to one's body with elbows locked against the body is helpful. I hold my breath as I'm shooting; others exhale slowly. Putting the camera in continuous shooting mode and taking several photos with the shutter release held down avoids the jerking that can occur with the first photo when pressing the shutter release. Practice helps.

Some butterflies, such as some satyrs, are spooked by the pre-flash that the flash uses to determine the necessary amount of light. This may cause the butterfly to fly off or flap its wings exactly when the photograph is being taken. There are a few ways to handle this situation. The most obvious is to shoot without a

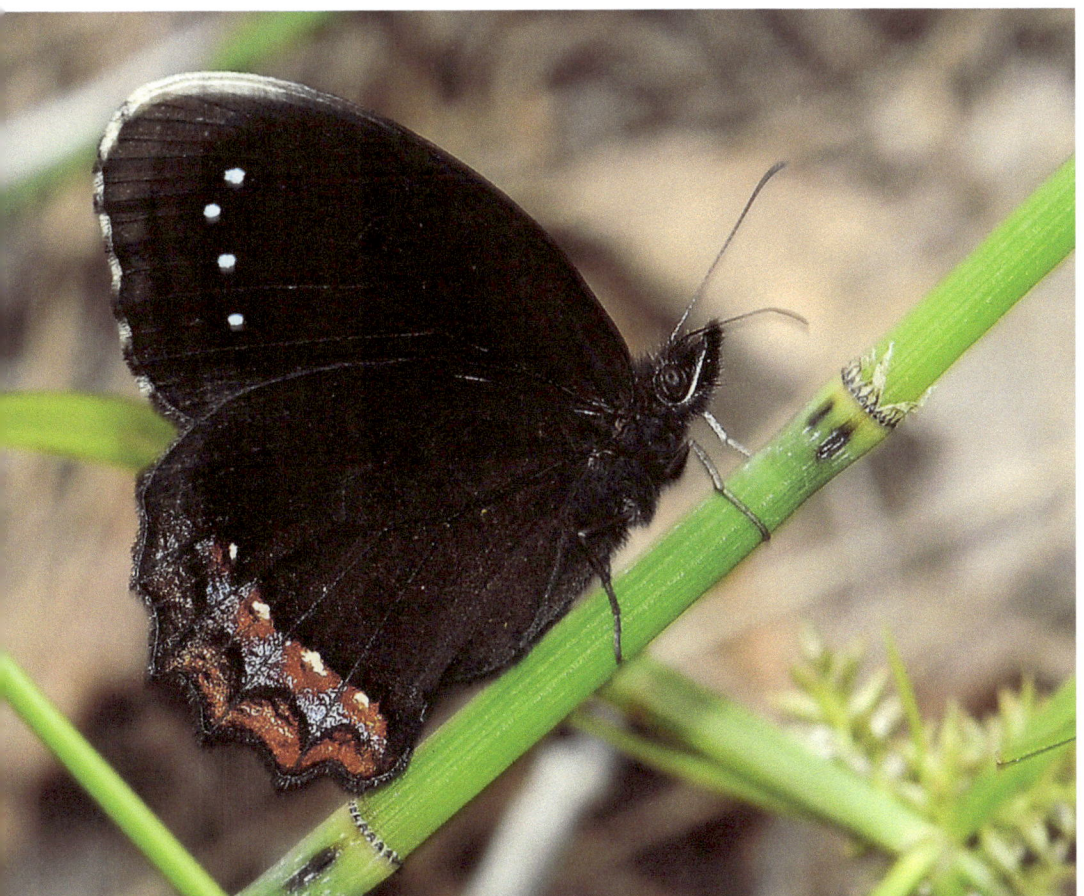

Red-bordered Satyr (*Gyrocheilus patrobas*). This butterfly occurs in wooded areas and is sensitive to light. It rests with its wings together, but flicks them open when hit with a pre-flash. In order to get this picture, I took three shots in rapid succession. The wings in the first photo were open and blurred. This was the second image. Photo taken in Ramsey Canyon, Arizona with a Nikon D300 camera, ISO 250, F11, 1/60 sec.

flash, but this is not always possible or desirable. If the butterfly only flaps its wings, then taking several photographs in rapid sequence may desensitize the butterfly to the flash. Alternatively, one can operate the flash in its manual mode in which case the pre-flash will not fire. It is worth practicing this in advance, to assess how much flash is needed for any given distance from the butterfly.

There is no need to get too close. Frame-filling photographs were often the goal with film cameras, but they are actually a disadvantage with digital photography. You want to leave room to crop the image in order to achieve the best photographic composition. Standing back also improves the depth of field. This is especially important when photographing a butterfly such as a skipper that lands with its forewings elevated 45 degrees. The purpose of the photograph also determines, in part, how close one needs to be. For identification purposes, it is more important to show the key field marks than to get close. If you are uncertain which field marks are important, try to photograph both the up-

per and lower wing surfaces, as well as the face and antennae.

Another difficult situation is trying to photograph a predominantly black butterfly. The light areas tend to be over-exposed as the camera and flash attempt to adequately expose the black color. The situation can be made worse because sunlight tends to bleach out the light areas. There are a couple of ways to avoid this problem. The easiest is to stand back and set the camera to meter off the entire frame. Alternatively, one can set the exposure compensation to -1 stop or more to "underexpose" the butterfly. For example, the Zebra Heliconian (*Heliconius charithonia*) is a black and yellow butterfly that is frustratingly difficult to photograph. This beautiful butterfly lands very briefly on flowers, giving the photographer little chance for a good shot. The black areas tend to cause the camera to overexpose the yellow bands, turning them white (see photos).

As mentioned earlier, I almost always use a fill flash, and occasionally, for dramatic effect, use

The Zebra Heliconian (*Heliconius charithonia*) is a black butterfly with pale yellow stripes. In the left photograph, the camera has attempted to render the black to be a more neutral gray and caused the butterfly to be overexposed. In the right photograph, the black color on the butterfly is underexposed, allowing the pale yellow in the butterfly's stripes to be visible. Both photographs taken in Everglades National Park. Left: Nikon Coolpix 990, ISO 100, F3.6, 1/160 sec, no flash. Right: Nikon Coolpix 8900 camera, ISO 50, F5.4, 1/450 sec.

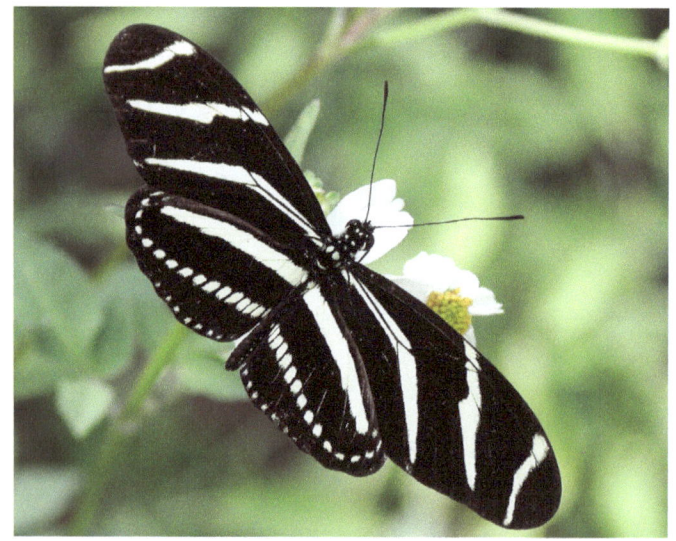 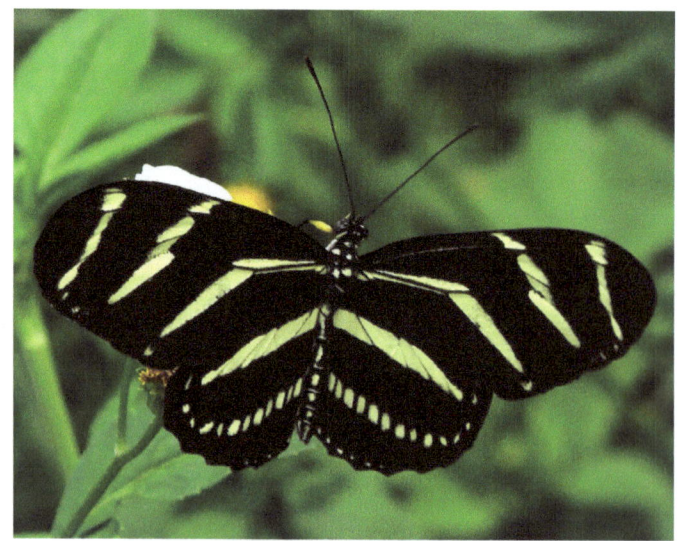

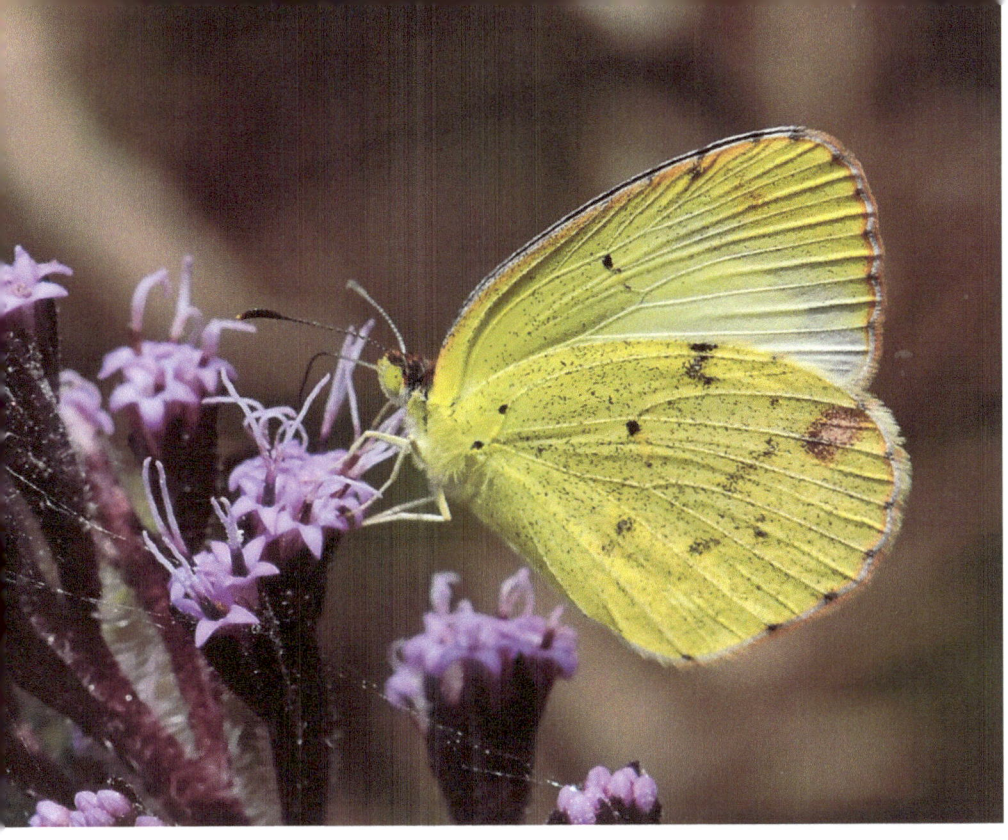

This photograph of a Little Yellow (*Eurema lisa*) was taken without a fill flash. Because of the butterfly's light color and white areas, a fill flash would likely overexpose the light-colored areas. Photo taken in Croatan National Forest, Craven County, North Carolina. Nikon D300 camera, 180 mm macro lens, ISO 800, F10, 1/1250 sec.

the flash as the sole light source against a dark background. However, there are times when the flash will make the photograph worse. The most common situation is when the sun is shining directly on a bright yellow butterfly, creating overexposed highlights. In this case, fill flash will make the highlights worse, and it is best to slightly underexpose the entire image.

Another advantage of a fill flash is that it allows one to photograph butterflies backlit by the sun, sometimes with dramatic effects. Sometimes the flash simply allows the "dark" side of the butterfly and flower to be properly illuminated. On the other hand, if the butterfly's wings are translucent, and the exposure compensation in the camera is reduced to darken the background, striking images can be obtained.

Clouded Sulphur (*Colias philodice*) backlit be the sun. This photo was taken in the late afternoon. Photo taken in Durham, North Carolina. Nikon Coolpix 8700 camera, ISO 50, F 5.1, 1/125 sec with SB-30 speedlight flash at 1/32 power.

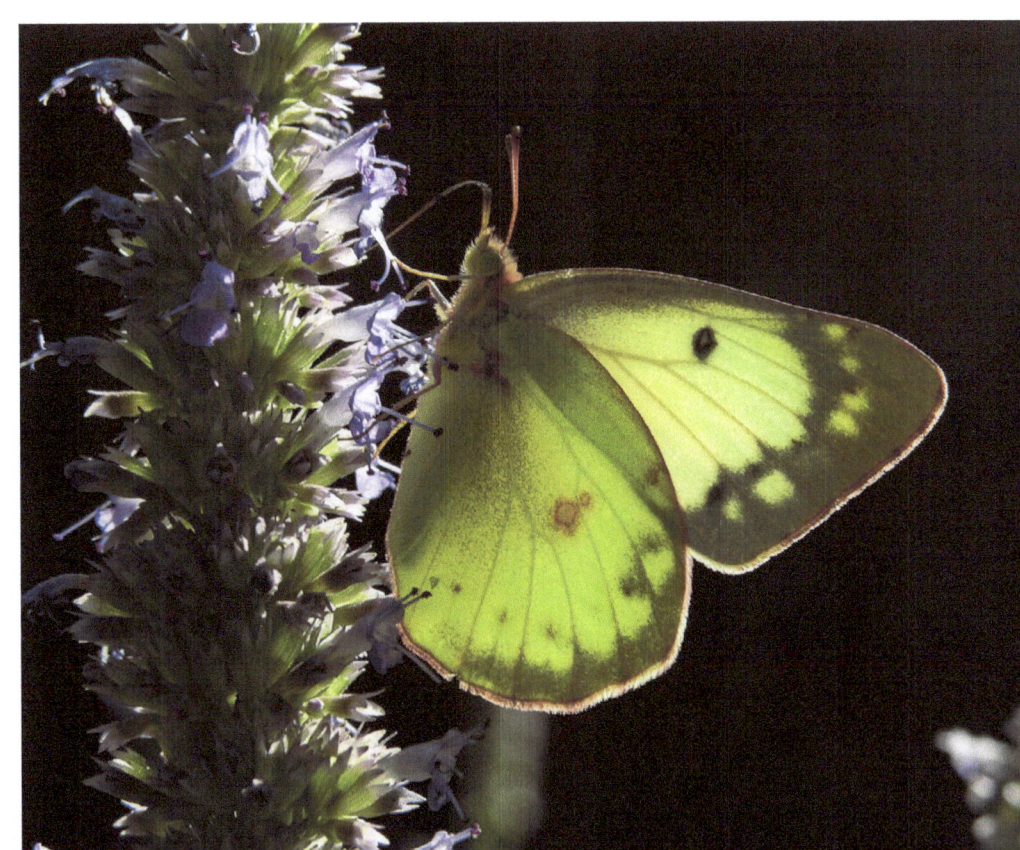

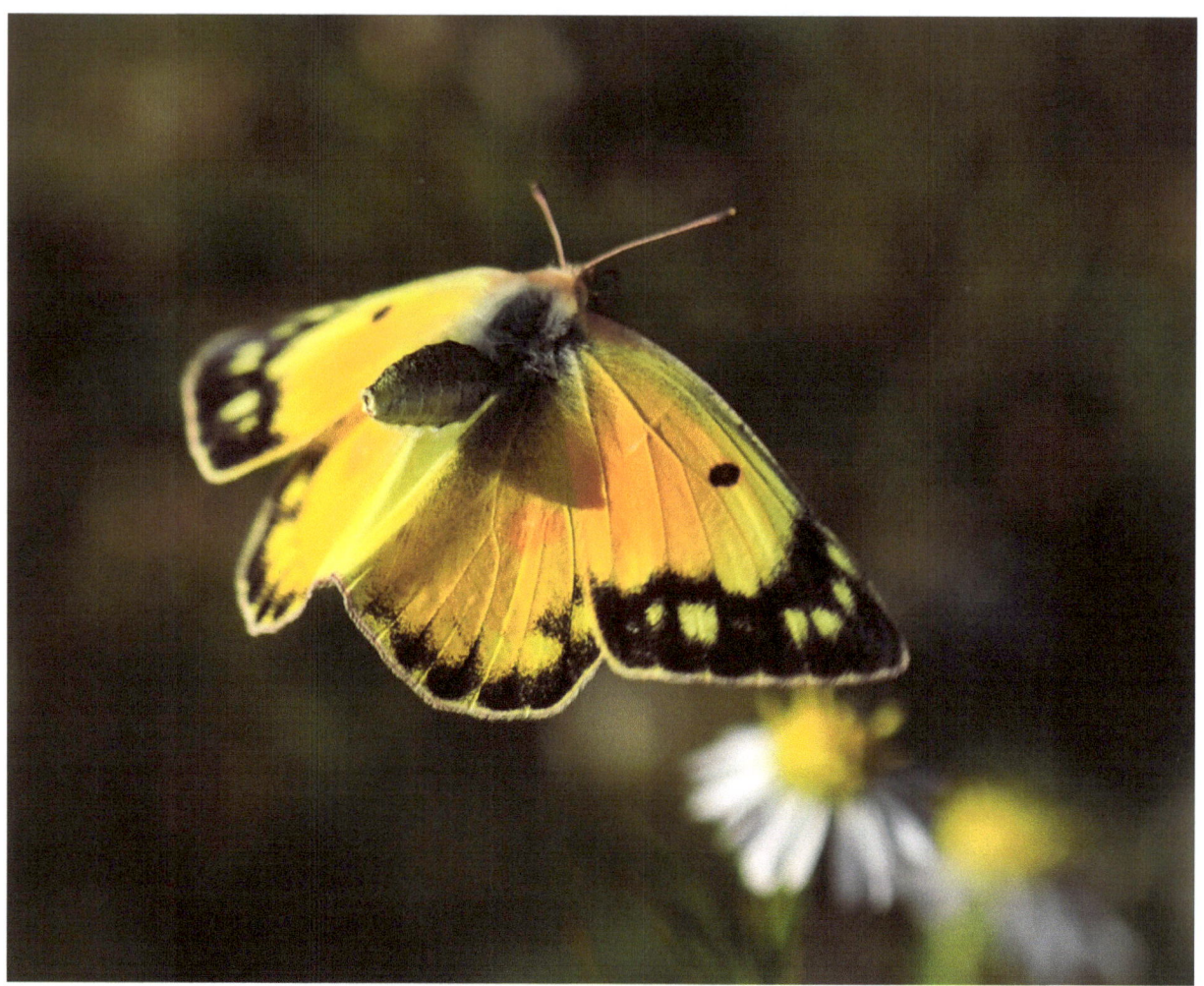

Orange Sulphurs (Colias eurythme) always land with their wings folded together, so the only way to photograph the upper side of the wing is to catch the butterfly in flight or photograph a dead one. In this photograph, there is minimal blurring of the right wings, because of the fast shutter speed and because the wings are at the end of a wing beat (the left wings are out of focus). If I were to take this photograph over again, I would have used a higher ISO, which would have allowed for a greater depth of field. The Nikon D300 camera was set on shutter priority, ISO 200, F3.5, 1/3200 sec.

A special situation exists when trying to photograph butterflies in flight. This is difficult to do for most butterflies. The same erratic flight that allows butterflies to avoid predators, makes it difficult to focus on them in flight. There are two situations where their flight is somewhat predictable. The first is a butterfly that is hopping from flower to flower. The second is during courtship when the male butterfly may hover above the female. In order to photograph a butterfly in either of these situations, one needs ample background light. In fact, it is best to turn off the flash, because the flash will not be able to overpower the ambient light. Even if it could,

a typical flash duration of 1/1000 second will not be short enough to freeze a butterfly's wings in flight. Next, the ISO should be increased to a very high value (2500 or 3200 on the Nikon D300 camera). In strong daylight, this will not usually cause discernable noise (see Page 28-9), especially if the camera has noise reduction software for high ISO settings. The camera should be set on shutter priority with a shutter speed as fast as the camera, lens and ambient light will allow (hopefully, 1/4000 to 1/8000 second). Finally, the shutter release should be set on the "continuous" mode, so that the camera keeps taking photos as long as the shutter release is pressed. The goal is to catch the butterfly with its wings fully extended. At this point the wings are transitioning between a down-beat and an up-beat and are the closest they will come to motionless.

Photographic Composition

The beauty of a butterfly photograph is in the eye of the beholder, and what pleases one observer may be different than another. Nevertheless, there are some guidelines that improve your chances of obtaining, or creating, a pleasing image. The first has already been mentioned: leave

room for cropping and/or rotating the photograph on a computer. No longer does one have to worry about perfectly level visual horizons or the positioning of the butterfly within the original image. Standing back also makes it easier to ensure that as much of the butterfly is in focus as possible.

If the butterfly lands with its wings closed, it's important to have the wings as parallel to the camera sensor as possible. This orientation will help to keep most of the butterfly in focus and preserve the shape of the wings. With a point and shoot camera with an articulating LCD

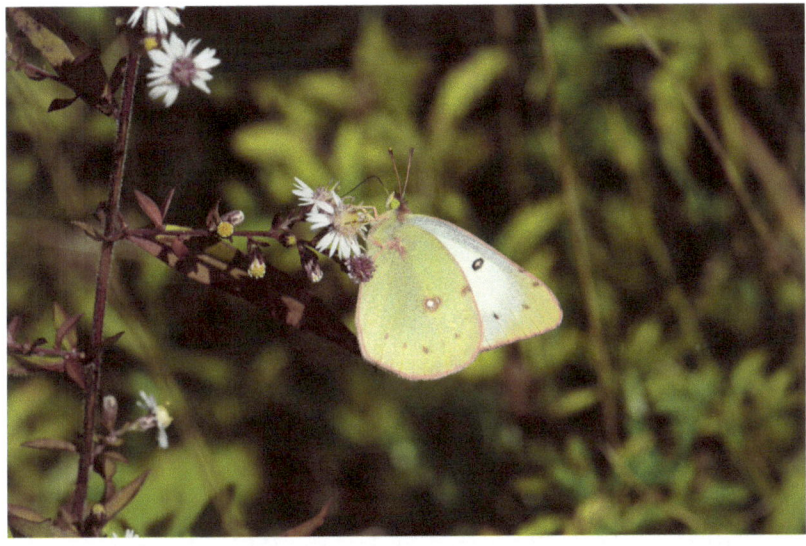

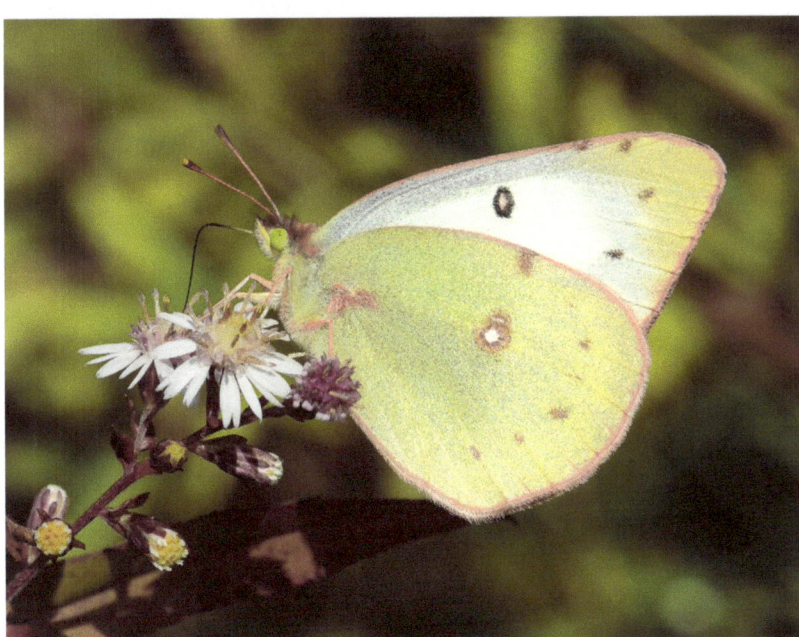

Clouded Sulphur (*Colias philodice*). The original photo on top is unremarkable with a "boring" central placement of the butterfly and a busy background. The cropped and rotated image on the bottom draws the viewer to the butterfly and de-emphasizes the background. Photo taken in Camden, Maine. Nikon D300 camera, , ISO 400, F11, 1/1250 sec, -0.3 exposure compensation on camera.

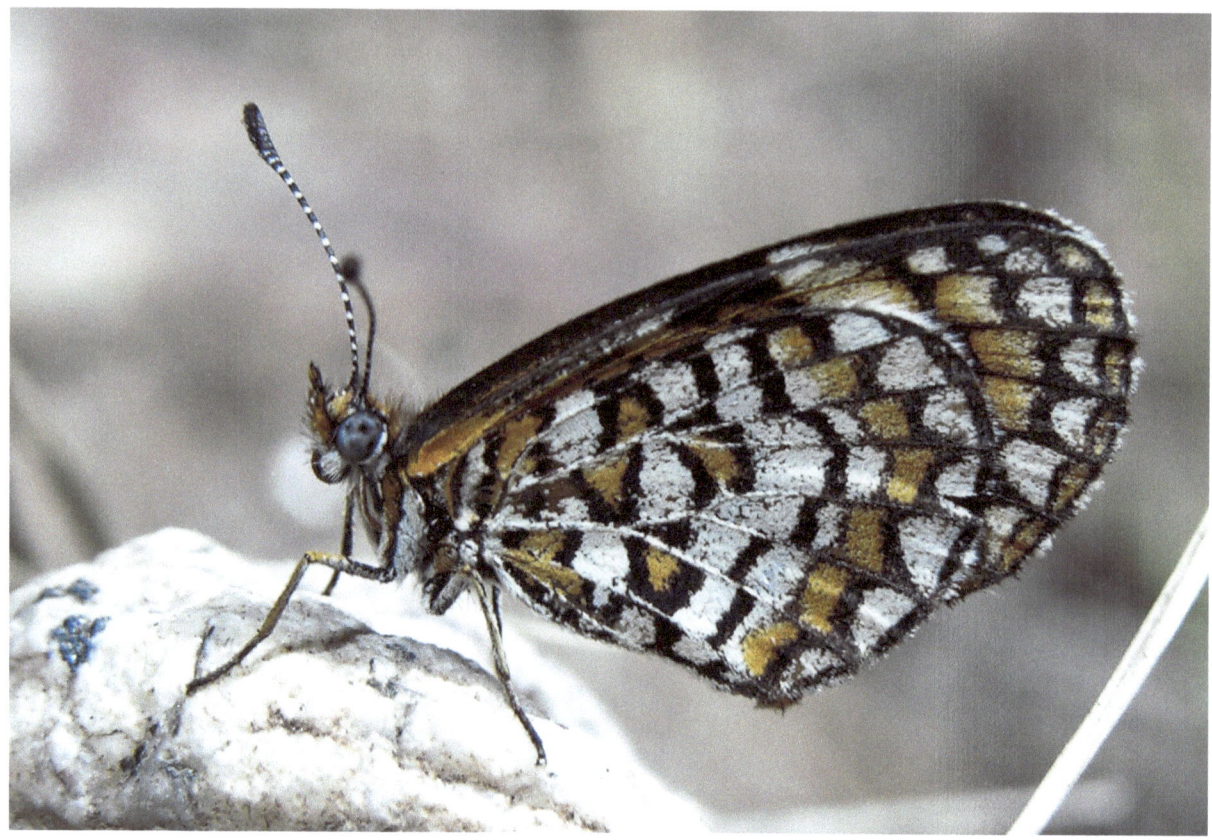

The placement and clarity of a butterfly's eyes can make or break a photograph. Although this image of a Tiny Checkerspot (*Dymasia dymas*) is technically good, it is the eyes, which are in focus and pointing at the photographer, that makes this a compelling photograph. Ideally, a butterfly's eyes should be visible, in focus, and not facing away from the photographer. At times, if the wings of a butterfly are spread out, most of the wings may be out of focus, but the photograph may still look good if the image of the eyes is crisp. Photo taken in Sabino Canyon, Arizona, with a Coolpix 8700 camera, ISO 50, F 5.8, 1/320 sec.

screen, this can be easily achieved by changing the orientation of the LCD screen with respect to the camera. With an SLR camera, the photographer must move, and this risks missing the photograph. In this situation, one usually takes a series of photographs, with the goal of eventually achieving the ideal orientation of the lens.

When the entire butterfly cannot be in focus, it is generally best to focus on the butterfly's head/eyes. Blurring of the wing edges often occurs, not only because the camera's sensor is not completely parallel to the wings, but also because some butterflies, such as hairstreaks, tend to move their wings back and forth. Another potential solution is to increase the depth-of-field by increasing the F stop in aperture-prior-

ity mode. This will mean shooting at a slower shutter speed, unless the ISO is increased at the same time. Alternatively, one can set the camera to manual mode, increase the F stop, and let the flash provide sufficient light. In this case, the flash may become the primary light source and the background will be darker.

For butterflies that land with their wings out flat, ideally the camera's sensor would again be parallel to the wings. Because it is often difficult to shoot from directly above the insect if it is oriented parallel to the ground, the best angle is slightly behind the butterfly. In front would be even better, but this is likely to cause a flight reaction. If the photograph is taken from the side, the wings will not be symmetrical, although this lack of symmetry does not necessarily detract from the photograph.

Grass skippers (small brownish skippers that use grasses as their host plants) can be identified from above or below, although identification is easiest from below as shown in the top photograph on this page. If a grass skipper lands with its wings open, the best orientation for photography is shown in the image at the bottom of the page.

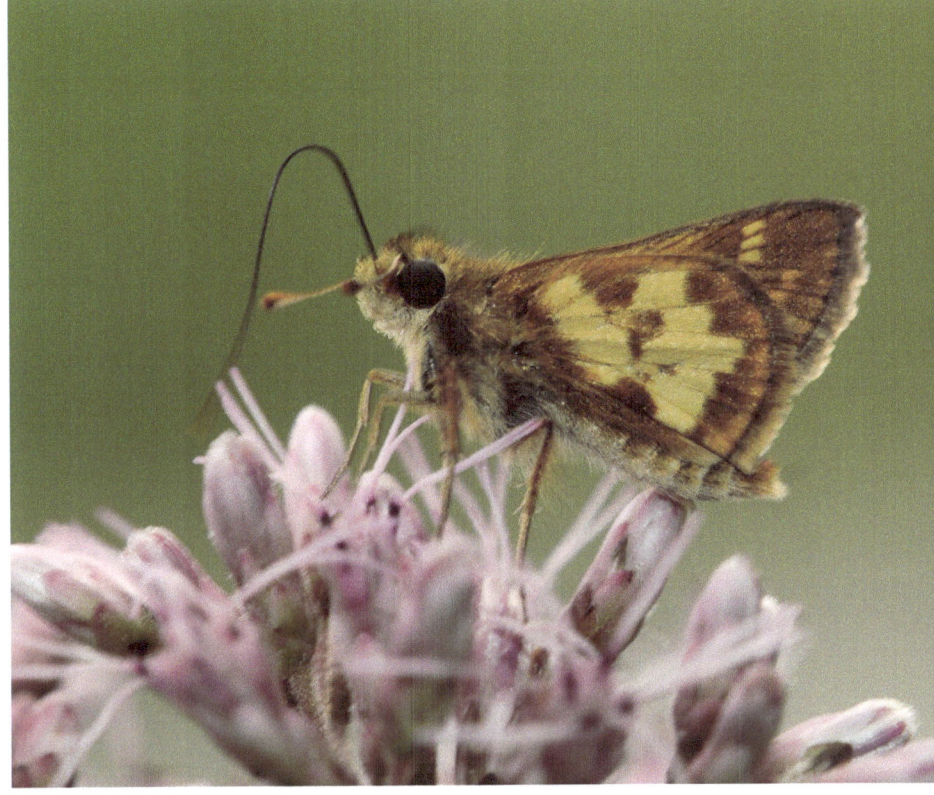

Peck's Skipper (*Polites peckius*). Many skippers are identified best with a side view showing the underside of the forewing and part of the hindwing, as in this photograph. Fortunately, when skippers land on flowers they usually do so with their wings closed together. Photo taken in Camden, Maine. Nikon D300 camera, ISO 200, F 10, 1/80 sec.

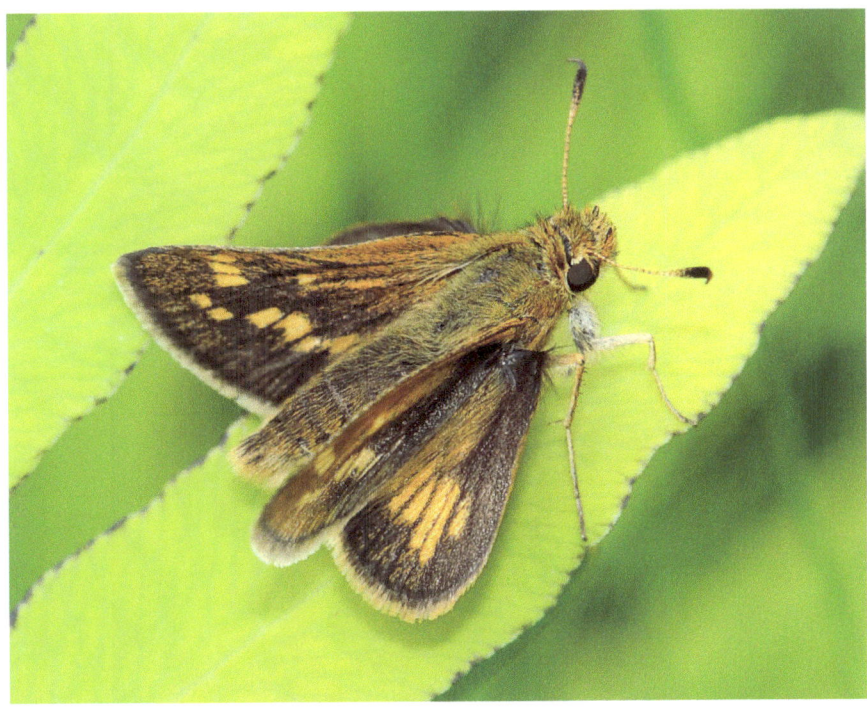

During cool parts of the day, many skippers open their wings to maximally absorb heat from the sun. This photograph shows the open-wing view of a Peck's Skipper (*Polites peckius*) showing the upper side of both the left forewing and the right hindwing. Such an orientation (from behind and to the side at about a 45 degree angle) is best for identification purposes. Photo taken in Camden, Maine. Nikon D300 camera, ISO 400, F 9, 1/200 sec.

Although butterflies are beautiful in their own right, some of the best photographs are obtained when the butterfly is matched with a flower. Not only does the flower add beauty to the photograph, it can balance the butterfly in both color and position, allowing the butterfly to be placed pleasingly off center in the photograph.

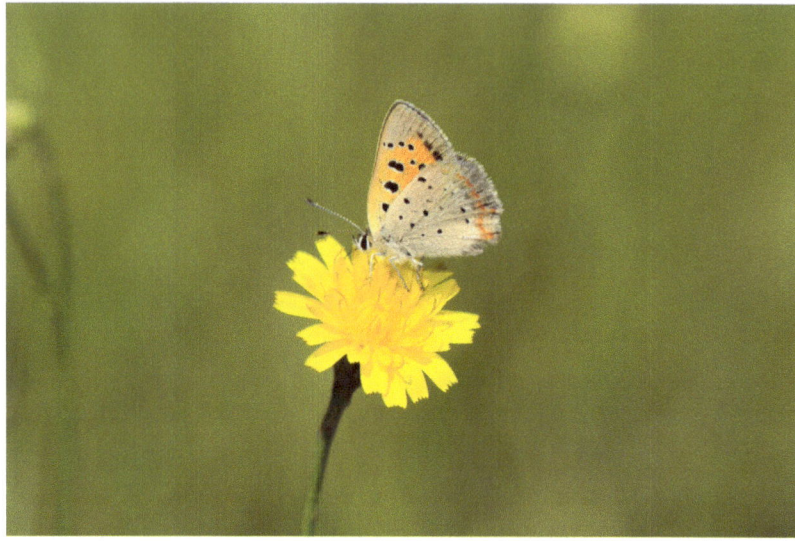

American Copper (*Lycaena phlaeas*) on a hawkweed. Top: original photo; Bottom: cropped and rotated image. In the cropped photo, the flower and butterfly are balanced, with roughly equal weighting for both. Note that the rotation of the image creates a better balance between the butterfly and flower. Photo taken in North Haven, Maine. Nikon D300 camera, ISO 200, F10, 1/400 sec.

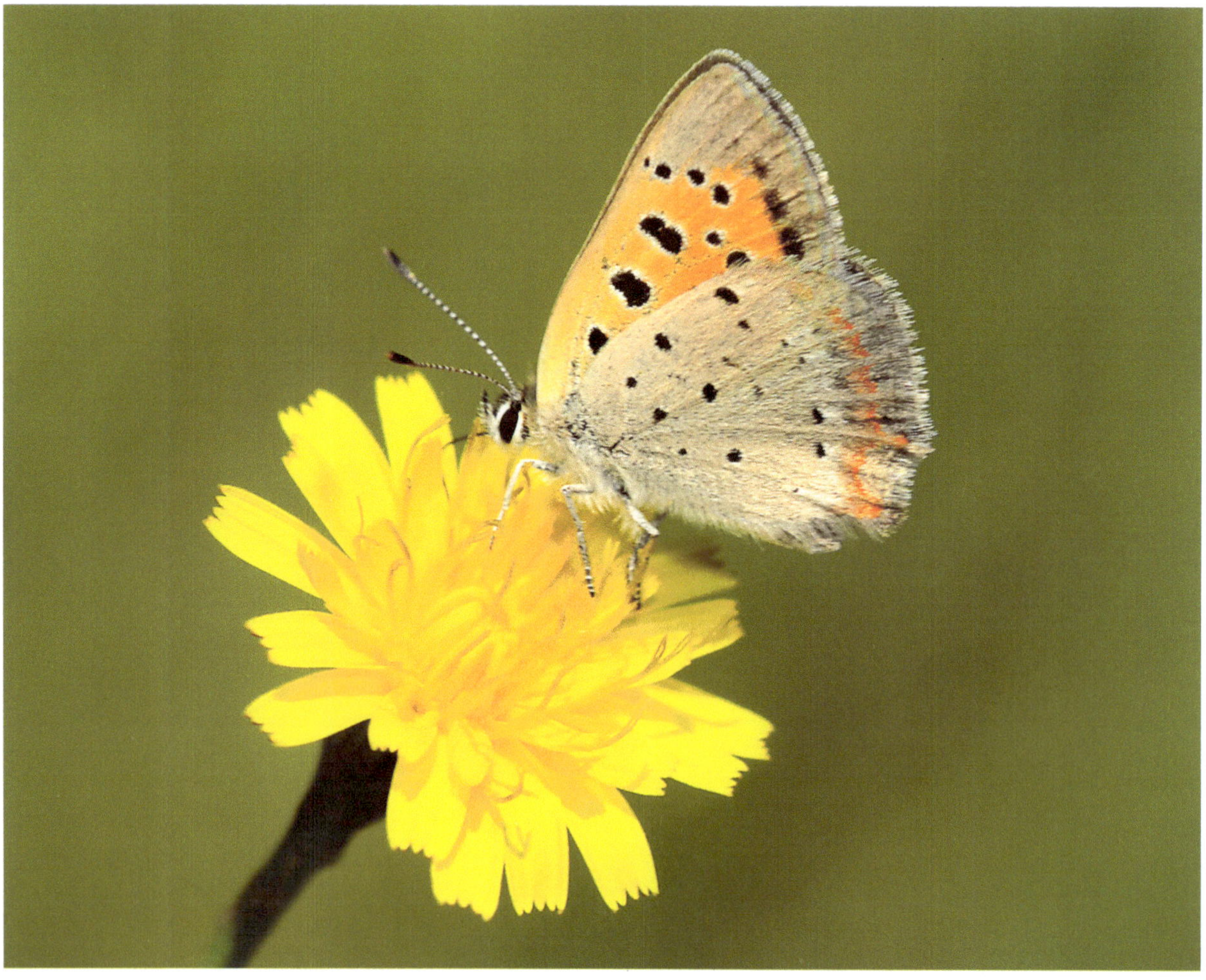

Putting a butterfly dead center in the photograph is generally suboptimal. It is usually best to follow the "rule of thirds." One divides the photograph into thirds horizontally and vertically. The intersections of the lines are the visual sweet spots, where the highlights of the photograph are best placed. In the figure below, the orange circles represent the sweet spots.

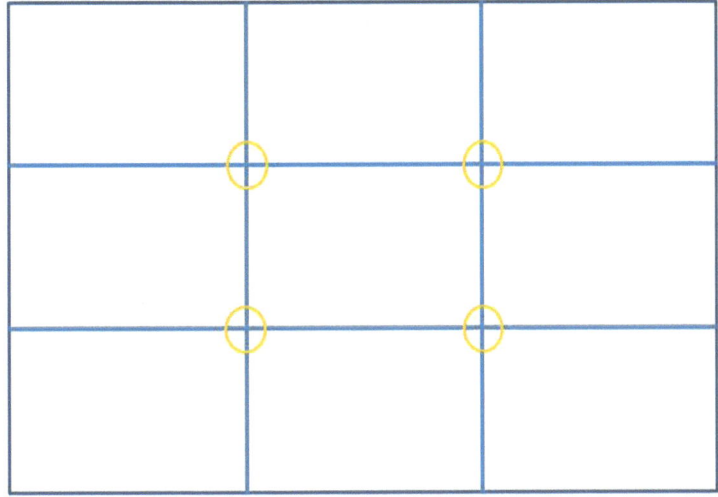

Diagramatic Representation of the "Rule of Thirds"

In the cropped photo of the American Copper on the previous page, both the butterfly and flower are centered on sweet spots in the image. On the other hand, the rule of thirds is only a guideline and there are obvious exceptions. For example, if the butterfly and its surroundings are symmetrical, often the butterfly fits naturally into the center, as shown in the image below of a Horace's Duskywing.

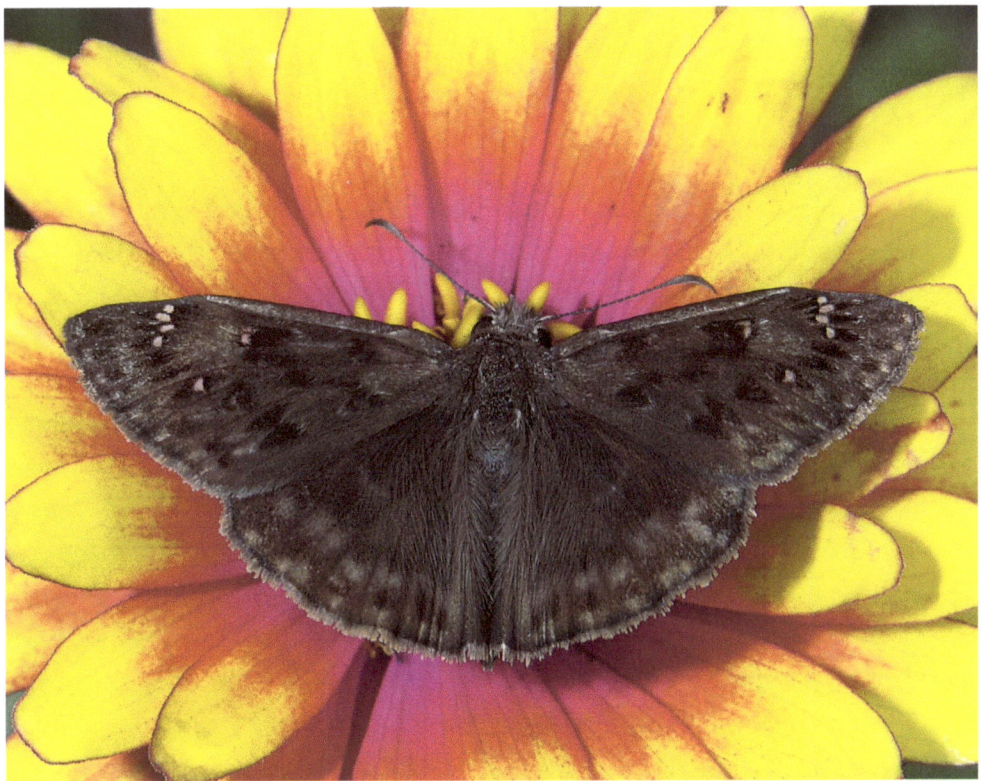

Horace's Duskywing (*Erynnis horatius*) on a Zinnia. Photo taken In Durham, NC. Coolpix 8700 camera, ISO 100, F 4.5, 1/120 sec.

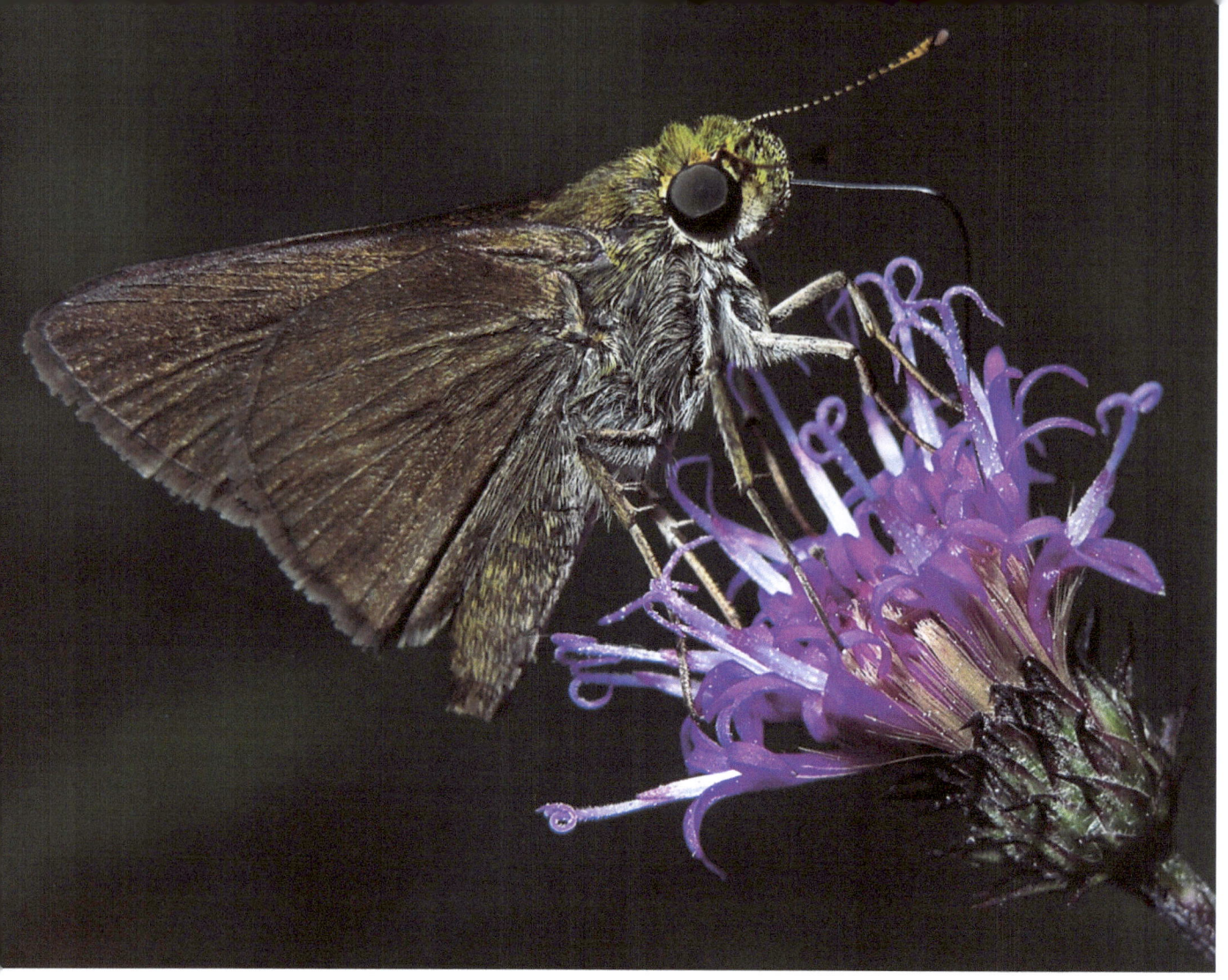

Dun Skipper (*Euphyes vestris*). The stem of the flower, arising from the corner of the image, forms a line that leads the viewer's eyes to the flower and butterfly. The flower is also part of the line that leads to the butterfly. Photo taken in Durham, North Carolina. Nikon Coolpix 8700 camera, ISO 50, F 4.5, 1/120 sec.

This image of the Horace's Duskywing illustrates two other key points. First, the butterfly should be placed so that its eyes look into the frame. In this image, the butterfly's head is near the center, so that the greatest "open" area of the photo is in front of the butterfly. The viewer is able to see what the butterfly sees. Second, the color of the butterfly is unremarkable, but the contrast of the butterfly with the brightly colored flower enhances the beauty of both.

Lines are an essential part of many butterfly photographs, whether they are straight or curved, or caused by sticks, stems, or the edge of a butterfly's wings. Lines that are parallel to the edge of the photograph are generally unexciting, where-

as diagonal lines can create a sense of movement and direction. Lines that arise from the corner of an image are particularly interesting, especially when they lead the eye to the main subject. One exception to these guidelines are horizons, which usually, when visible, should be parallel to the top edge of the photograph.

Lines that detract from an image are ones that cross the butterfly's wings. These may blades of grass or shadows cast from surrounding vegetation. Some butterflies, such as the Georgia Satyr (*Neonympha areolata*), habitually land in dense grass, making them very difficult to photograph. And no matter how much flash one uses, it is impossible to obliterate a shadow on

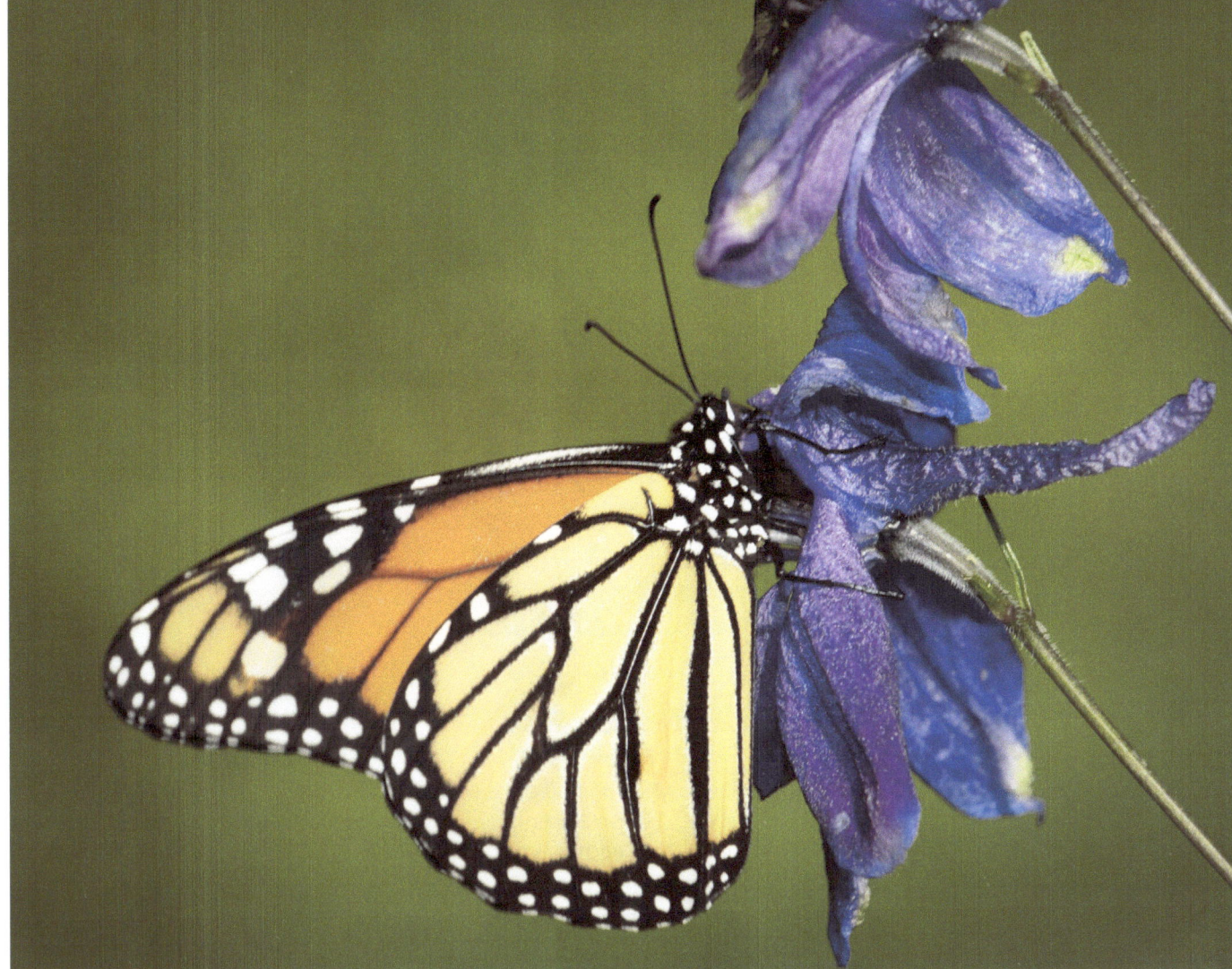

Monarch (*Danaus plexippus*) on Larkspur. The lines here add interest to an already attractive photograph. The two parallel flower stems lead the viewer's eyes into the image and over the butterfly. Secondly, the edge of the butterfly's upper (fore) wing leads back to the lower stem, forming an arc, and up to the spur of the lower flower, forming a reverse curve. Photo taken in Camden, Maine with Nikon D300, ISO 250, F11, 1/320 sec.

a butterfly's wing. Although soft late afternoon light is generally more pleasing than strong mid-day light, there are more shadows late in the day, making butterfly photography more difficult.

Thus far we have discussed the main subject(s) in an image, but the background and foreground are equally important. The background should be uncluttered, so as not to detract from the image. Bright, busy backgrounds distract the viewer. One disadvantage of point and shoot cameras is that the depth of field is so great that it is hard to blur the background. The photo-graph of the Monarch above is enhanced by the simplicity of the background, due to it being out of focus, and absence of any distracting fore-ground. In contrast, the busy background of the photo on top of the next page detracts from an otherwise pleasing image. This could have been avoided, to some extent, by shooting in aperture-priority at the lowest F-stop possible, which results in a narrower depth of field.

Another way to unclutter a background is to use the flash as the main source of light, creating a dark background. There are several ways to do this, depending on the camera set-up, but basically the combination of shutter speed and aperture are set to underexpose the background with the flash providing sufficient light to the subject. This presupposes that there is sufficient distance between the subject and background

Mated pair of Eastern Tailed-Blues (*Everes co-myntas*). This image is filled with interesting, symmetrical curves: the blade of grass support-ing the butterflies, the arc created by the joined abdomens, the rounded curves of the butter-flies' wings. But how much better would this photo have been if the background had been uniform and non-dis-tracting? Photo taken in Durham, North Carolina, with Nikon Coolpix 8700 ISO 50, F6, 1/400 sec.

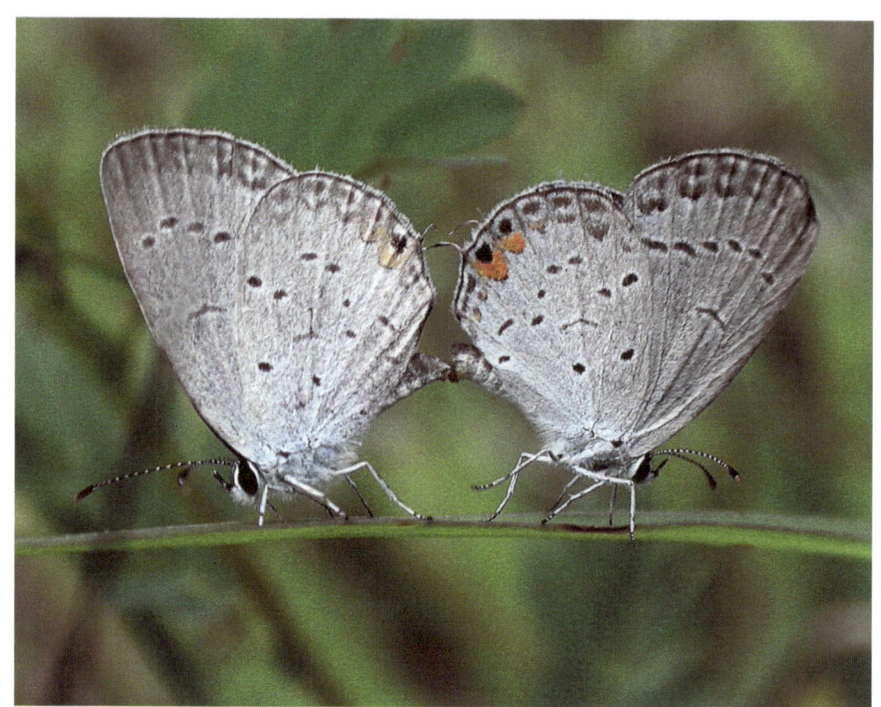

In this photo, the Gulf Fritillary (*Agraulis vanillae*) is separated from the background not only by using a telephoto lens, but also by setting the camera to underexpose the image, forcing the flash to become the primary source of light. Photo taken in Beaufort, North Carolina with Nikon D300, ISO 500, F 10, 1/500 sec, -0.7 exposure compensation on the camera.

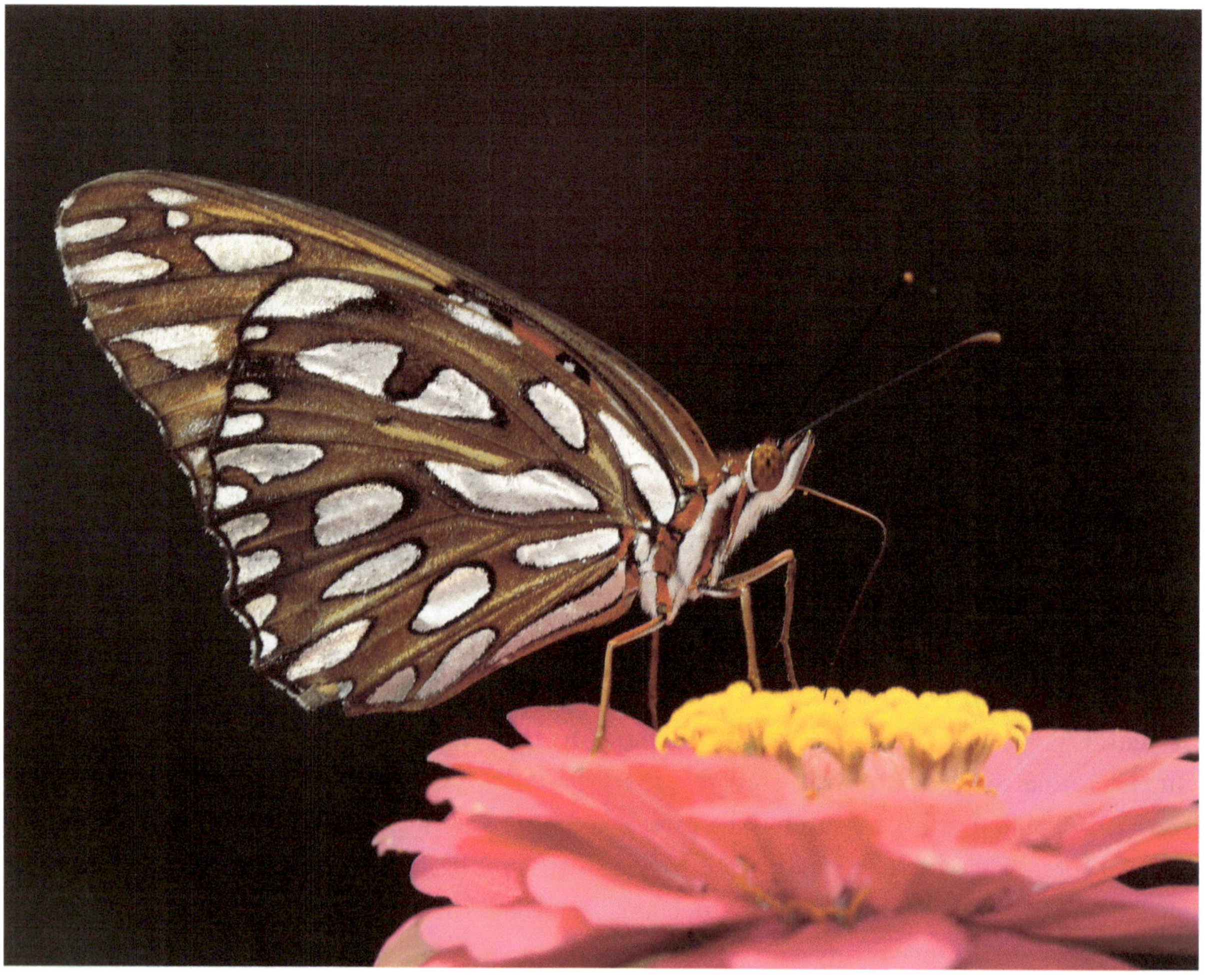

to light the subject without lighting the background. When the flash is used in this manner, a diffuser should be used to minimize the harshness of light from the flash.

In general, foregrounds are best avoided where possible. This is not possible if a butterfly is sitting on the ground or on a leaf, but the foreground can be minimized by appropriate cropping. Occasionally, a foreground enhances an image with lines that interact well with the subject or lead the viewer's eyes towards the subject.

Color, of course, is an important part of butterfly photography. Contrasting colors can separate a butterfly from the background and are especially important when the background is close to the butterfly (see, for example, the American Copper on of Page 19 or the Golden-headed Scallopwing on Page 22). Complementary colors in a butterfly and flower can also enhance the beauty of both. Examples of

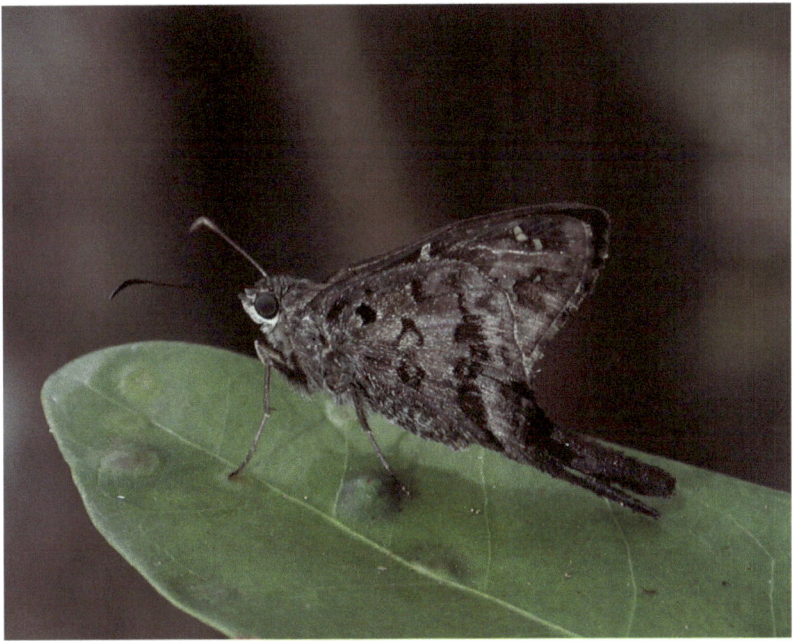

Dorantes Longtail (*Urbanus dorantes*). One of the few instances (among my photographs) where the foreground adds to the picture. Here the midrib of the leaf parallels the abdomen and tail of the butterfly, and both the leaf and butterfly are "looking" in the same direction. Photo taken in Everglades National Park. Nikon Coolpix 990 camera, ISO 100, F 3.2, 1/130 sec.

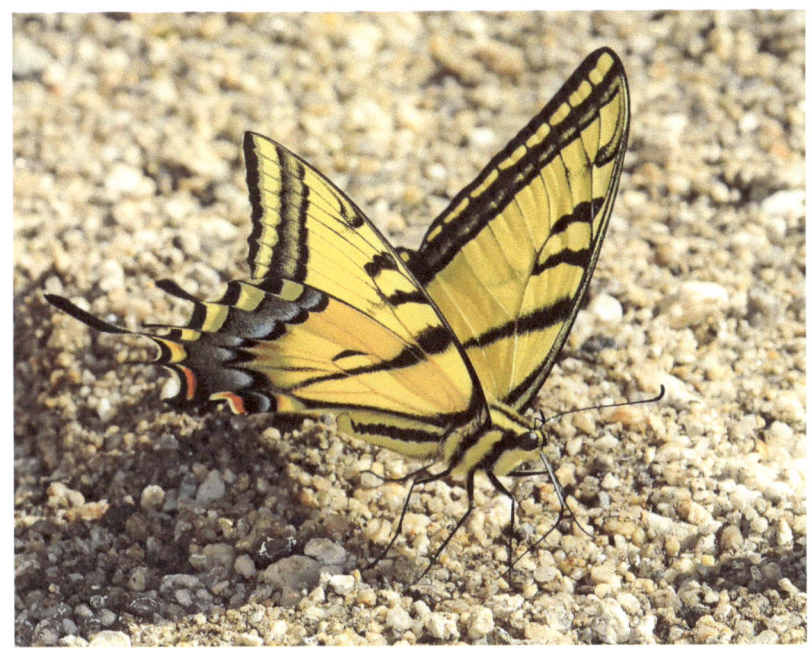

Two-tailed Swallowtail (*Papilio multicaudata*). In this photograph the foreground was minimized by cropping the image close to the butterfly's legs. Photo taken in Sierra Vista, Arizona. Nikon D300, ISO 400, F 11, 1/800 sec.

complementary colors are purple and yellow, or red and green (see, for example, the photo of the Cloudless Sulphur and Morning Glory on Page 18). Another pleasing combination occurs when the color of the flower is the same as a minor color of the butterfly, as in the Red-banded Hairstreak on Page 18). However, unless one plants flowers that will go well with a butterfly known to fly in that location, taking a photograph with a compelling color combination entails repeated effort and some luck.

Storing and Sharing Images

In the urge to take pictures, often too little thought is given to the electronic storage of the images. First, it is essential to have at least two back-ups of any important photographs. Hard drives crash, usually at inopportune times, and often their contents cannot be retrieved. I synchronize my desktop computer with a laptop used for travel, and each computer has its own external back-up drive. The most secure approach is to have an additional copy of the images stored online. While writing this book, I e-mailed the text to myself each evening to ensure that the latest version was retrievable online.

Just like any library, it is important to have a catalog (folder) system for storing photographs. It helps to add keywords or "tags" to a photograph or set of photos to make them easier to retrieve. Windows Live Photo Gallery or Iphoto on Macintosh computers can add the tags or search for photographs using titles, dates or keywords. Similarly, many other programs such as Adobe Bridge (part of Photoshop) and Adobe Lightroom (another image processing software program) have this capability.

There are many photo sharing sites, such as Flickr, on the web. These make it easy for anyone to see your photographs, but one word of caution. Images can be downloaded from most of these sites, even if you've given instructions for them not to be downloadable. If you don't want viewers to have access to the original photographs, upload only smaller files of the photos.

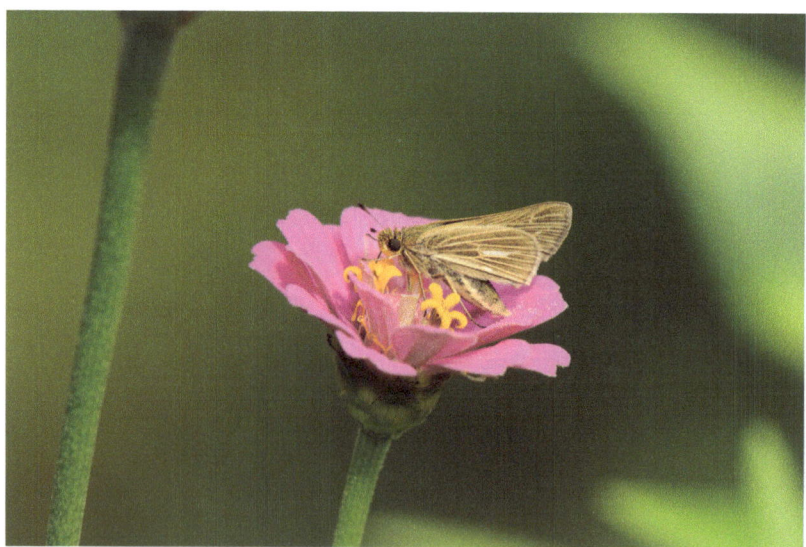

This is an image that came from my camera. Although the Saltmarsh Skipper (*Panoquina panoquin*) and Zinnia make a pleasing combination, the background is distracting with an extraneous stem on the left and some light areas on the right and top. I also would prefer a more conventional 8x10 image to hang on my wall. Photo taken in Beaufort, North Carolina. Nikon D300 Camera, Tamron 180 mm macro lens, ISO 500, F10, 1/400 sec.

Modifying the Image

You've captured the picture – now what? The advent of digital photography means that the computer has become the darkroom. No longer does one need a host of special equipment. All that is required is the computer you already have and an image processing program. However, the potential to improve a photograph is almost limitless, and hours in the darkroom have now morphed into hours on the computer. There are many excellent "how to" books on the market, and instructions on the use of programs such as Adobe Photoshop and Lightroom are beyond the scope of this book. On the other hand, starting with the photo on the previous page, I will show some of the simple things one can do to enhance the image from the camera.

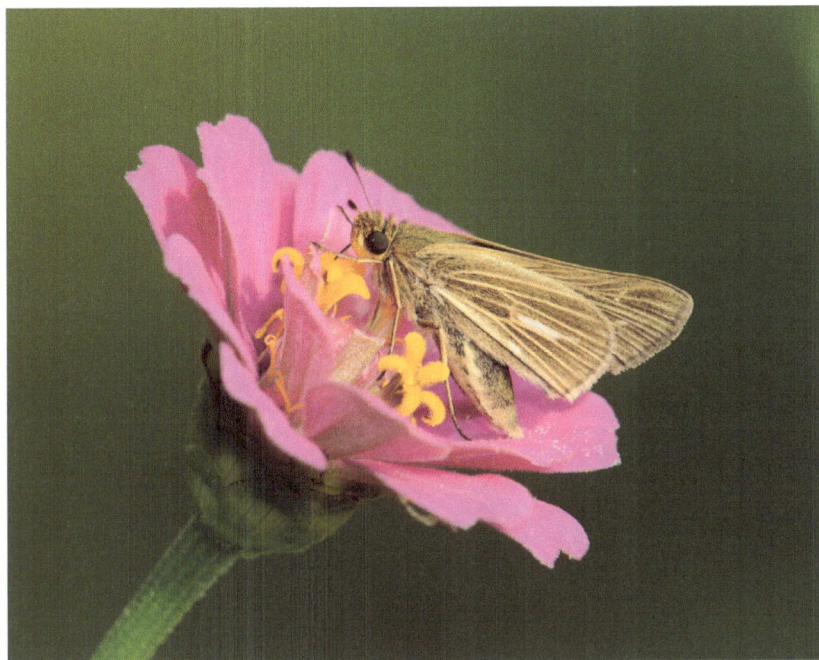

By rotating and cropping the photo, the stem now forms a diagonal line leading to the flower and butterfly. The distractions in the background are cropped out, and the image is more focused on the flower and butterfly.

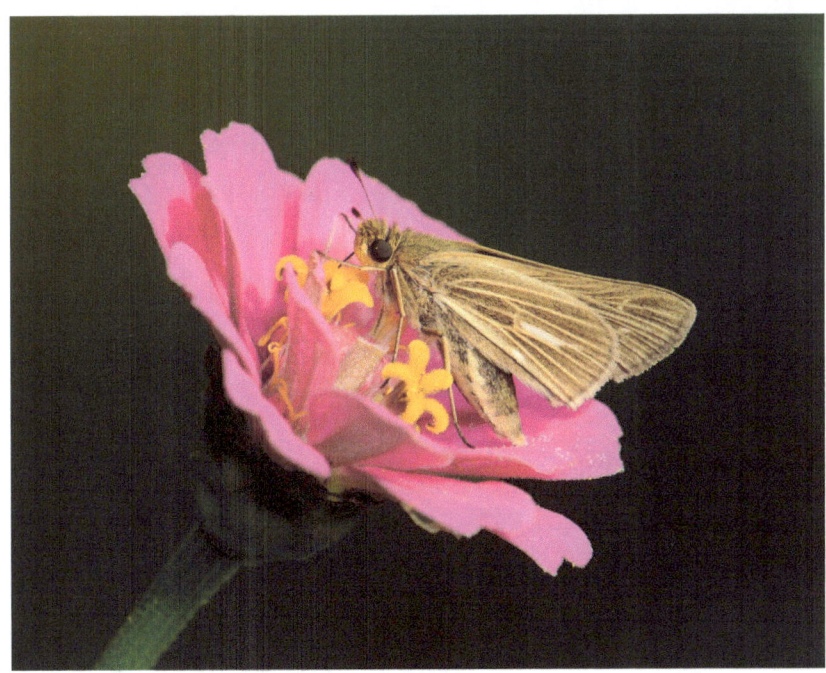

Now, for the sake of demonstration, let's say that I wanted to make the separation of the flower and butterfly from the background even greater. I could darken the background and increase the saturation of the pink in the flower.

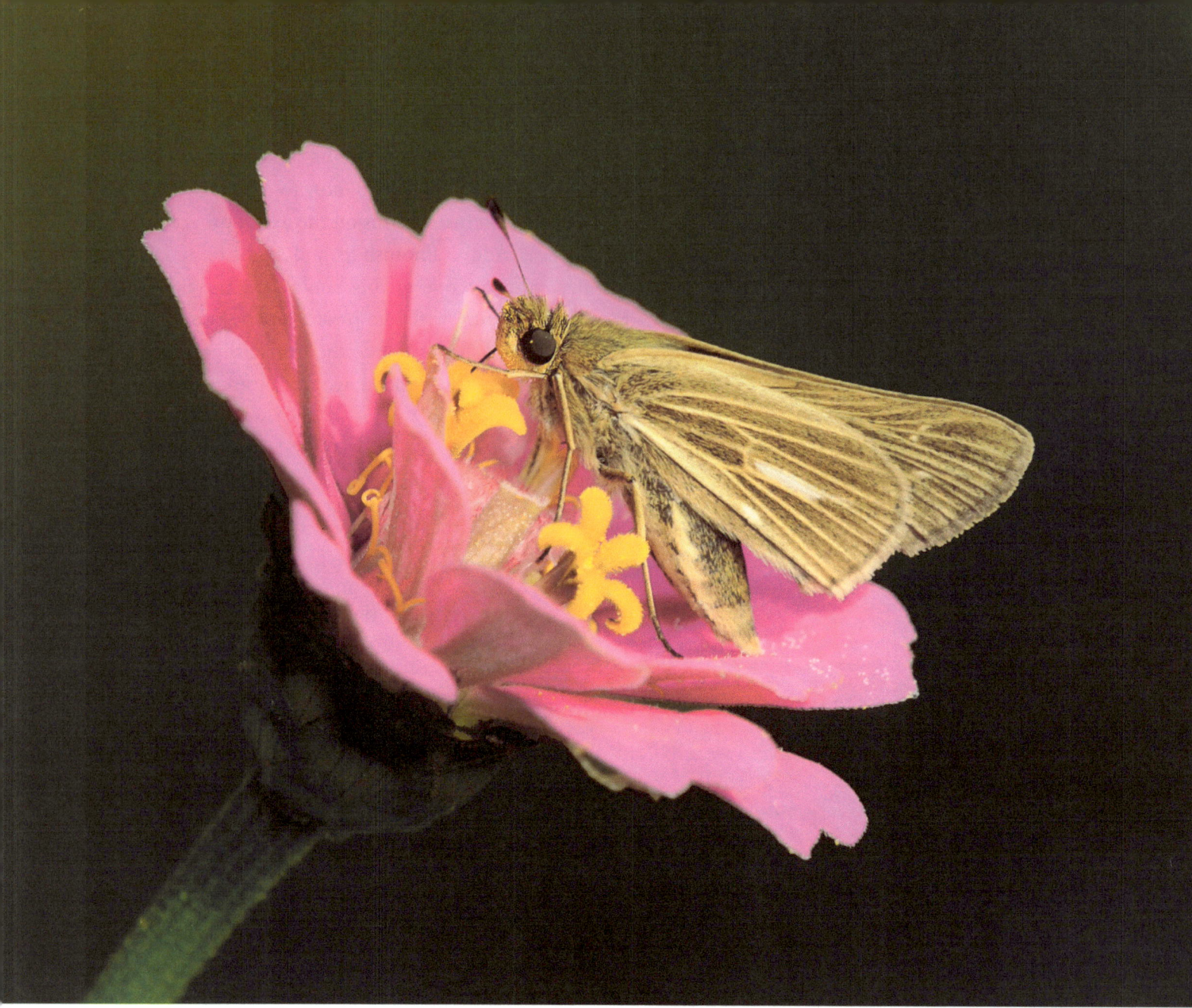

The most important focal point in the image is the butterfly's eyes. All digital photographs are inherently a bit blurry due to the fact that pixels can only contain one value, even if there is a change in color or light intensity within that pixel. There are programs that can enhance the contrast between adjacent areas, removing some of the blurring, but such programs can also make both noise and tiny defects in the color of a butterfly more visible. Therefore, although I can sharpen the entire photograph, all that I really want sharp is the butterfly's head, as I have done in the image on this page.

The critical viewer will see the defects in pink color (white blotches) in the flower petal just to the right of the tip of the butterfly's abdomen. In an image processing program, these defects could be replaced with the pink color nearby using a cloning tool.

The purpose of this demonstration is to provide an introduction to the myriad of adjustments that can be made to a photograph. In reality, I would be happy with just rotating and cropping the initial photo, but one can also spend hours on a photograph, creating something that verges on painting.

Conclusion

If you've slogged through this book up to this point, you must be breathing a sigh of relief. Almost done! But in reality, this is only the beginning of your (and my) continued exploration into nature photography. If you're a novice photographer, the learning curve will be steep, and it's important not to get discouraged when the images you've taken are not as good as you had hoped – most of the time for me. If you're an experienced photographer, hopefully I've been able to give you a few new ideas. You probably know techniques and strategies that I have not discussed, and I also welcome the opportunity to learn from you. Finally, we need to pay homage to the power of luck. For example, the photograph on this book's cover was enhanced, I think, by some leaves that were waving out of focus in the foreground beneath the butterfly. For the images of butterflies ovipositing (laying eggs) on their host plants, I did not know that's what they were doing when I took the photographs.

Undoubtedly, technical advances in digital photography will make parts of this book obsolete in the not-too-distant future. My goal is to keep updating a digital edition to keep pace with these changes. On the other hand, the beauty of a good photograph is everlasting. I wish you the same thrill and satisfaction with butterfly photography that I have experienced over the last 15 years.

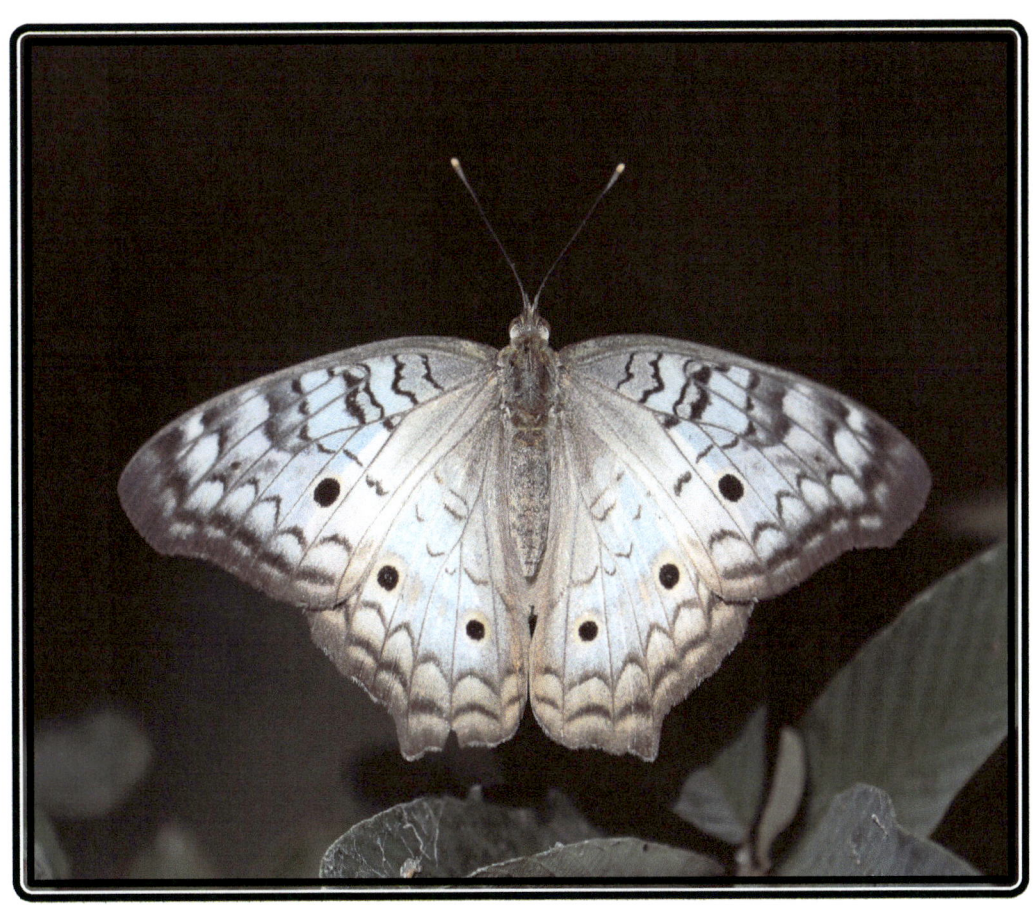

Index